THE
DIVERSITY
PLAYBOOK

|

TRANSFORMING BUSINESS

WITH INCLUSION AND INNOVATION

|

BY

HEPHZI PEMBERTON

Copyright © Hephzi Pemberton 2021

The right of Hephzi Pemberton to be identified as the Author
of the Work has been asserted by her in accordance with
the Copyright, Designs and Patents Act 1988.

Author: Hephzi Pemberton, Equality Group; www.equality.group

Editor and Author Coach: Wendy Yorke,
WRITE. EDIT. PUBLISH; www.wendyyorke.com

Publisher: Serapis Bey Publishers, USA; www.parulagrawal.com

Design: Rebekka Mlinar

The acknowledgments on pp. ix constitute an extension
of this copyright page.

This book is for information about Diversity and Inclusion, it is for
strategic and educational purposes only and is not intended to act
as a substitute for professional advice or consultancy. Any person
requiring additional information or professional services should
consult a verifiable provider, such as the Equality Group.

A CIP catalogue record for this title is available from the British Library

Paperback ISBN 978-1-7370403-1-6

This book is dedicated to everyone who is working
for a brighter, kinder and bolder future.
Keep believing, keep persevering and keep welcoming
others into that vision.

ACKNOWLEDGEMENTS

I am deeply grateful for the support and inspiration of my family, friends and colleagues.

Thank you to my parents who have always modelled hard work and a deep social ethic throughout my life. To my four siblings, Seth, Phoebe, Imogen and Benedict, who make family endless fun and a lifelong adventure. To my son Max who has expanded my heart and taught me the beauty of the moment. To Barney who has supported me through several evenings and weekends of writing. He is always happy to listen to chapter drafts and bring me tea on longer days. A true partner, who I am eternally grateful for.

Thank you to the Equality Group team who are by far the most committed, talented, energetic and visionary group I have ever had the pleasure of working with. I love seeing your faces on a Monday morning and collaborating with you on all the incredible projects we have the privilege to work on.

Finally, thank you to Wendy Yorke for your wise guidance, thoughtful edits and constructive feedback. Your constant belief that I could write *The Diversity Playbook* within the timeframe and with all the additional responsibilities of business building and motherhood was a guiding light.

PRAISE FOR
THE DIVERSITY PLAYBOOK

"This is the essential playbook for building an inclusive workplace. Beyond attracting and hiring diverse talent, this book features how to develop, promote and retain talent from all backgrounds. A must-read for leaders who wish to bridge the gap between surviving and thriving in the modern workplace."
Dr Lisa Shu, Executive Director, Newton Venture Program

"The Diversity Playbook is a must-read for business leaders wanting to make real impact in their organisation. Well-written, easy to understand and filled with examples, actionable reflections and exercises, the book provides an evidence-based approach to increasing diversity across any organisation. By referencing recent studies and data in the diversity space, it gives a swift summary of the why, who and how, for anyone interested in the topic. Hephzi Pemberton writes from the perspective of a practitioner, both as a senior recruiter and diversity advisor, but also having been a business leader and serial entrepreneur herself."
Vivian Bertseka, Founding Partner, Just Climate

"Combining years of experience and deep research, The Diversity Playbook is a fantastic resource for anyone looking for practical steps to advance inclusion in their organisation."
David Rossow, Strategic Investor, Board Advisor

"A necessary and timely treatment of a real and pressing issue. Hephzi Pemberton takes scientific research and distils it into relevant and practical advice for the business world."
Dr Keon West, Reader Social Psychology, Goldsmiths University of London, Head of Research, Equality Group

"We know diversity is good for business. *The Diversity Playbook* tells you how to turn the theory into reality. This book is for every founder and business leader who wants to compete for the best talent and create a culture where everyone can thrive."
Emma Sinclair MBE, CoFounder, EnterpriseAlumni, UNICEF advisor

"If you want to understand how to make your organisation more diverse and inclusive, but don't know where to start, read this book. Clear and concise and based on the latest research, *The Diversity Playbook* is an essential guide to transforming your business."
Matthew Green, Author, former Financial Times correspondent

"Hephzi Pemberton's key message in *The Diversity Playbook* is that organisations which embrace diversity will ultimately do better. They will be able to create more wealth for their employees and shareholders as a result of the greater creativity that comes with greater inclusion. I wholeheartedly agree with her and with her assertion that, although there are now more women and ethnic minorities acting as Non-Executive Directors on company boards, there are still far too few in senior management roles. Part of the issue is that woman and executives from ethnic minorities do not have the confidence to put themselves forward for senior roles and it is incumbent on all of us to encourage them to do so. As she says, 2020 was a watershed year and we need to learn lessons from it and fight for greater diversity and inclusion in all parts of our society."
Nicola Horlick, CEO of Money & Co

"As sustainable investors, we recognise that diversity, equity and inclusion drive performance and that barriers limit potential. We think management teams can achieve huge impact through their focus here. *The Diversity Playbook* is a great place to start."
Alina Manolache, Director, Generation Investment Management

FOREWORD
THE DIVERSITY PLAYBOOK IS TIMELY AND NECESSARY.

In April 2021, I was interviewed by CNBC, Financial Times, Forbes Magazine, Inc. Magazine and they have all asked me, "What is the current state of diversity and inclusion?" In fact, the writer from Forbes inquired about the latest iteration, which is justice, equity, diversity and inclusion. Here is the deal, it does not matter what we call the workforce diversity phenom, formerly known as diversity and inclusion. What matters is understanding the context surrounding the problem and accepting that there is a need for a paradigm shift before you can be open to the solutions that this playbook offers. My response to the question on the state of diversity is that we are amid a global reckoning of racism that has emboldened the people to protest and inspired a major shift in the way international businesses address underrepresented groups, such as women, and people with visible and invisible differences.

Even the most conservative industries, from financial services to the adolescent tech industries, have spoken out against racism for the first time. The genesis was a race-based protest triggered by the murder of an African-American man, named George Floyd. What ensued across the world, as millions joined the protest and spoke out against injustice, shifted the way businesses began to reprioritise diversity. Depending on which side of the pond you reside, you may not agree that this is a global matter, but the people have spoken out in protest and demanded attention to racism and discrimination, particularly in policing, but also in the workplace.

Now that we have unprecedented global attention on diversity, we have to consider how do we move the needle? We have to reconsider and re-imagine how we look at diversity and what actions create the impact we want to see. To do that we need to disrupt our ways of thinking, unlearn old habits and adopt new ways of being together with the unique perspectives provided by thought leaders who stretch us and make us uncomfortable for the good and betterment of the world we live in. Hephzi Pemberton is one such voice. She is the woman and I am proud to see her step up and grab the megaphone in The Diversity Playbook.

We need the bold and courageous voices of today's thought leaders to speak to the issues around diversity, but also to highlight the new nuances with respect to homogeneous groups and the issue of gender diversity, which is still unsolved and being challenged. I agree with Hephzi when she writes that "... a group of White women lack diversity exactly as much as a group of White men". Hephzi is going to the uncomfortable and the challenging places and offering us ways of seeing, being and doing things differently. In this excellent book, she explores the idea that is a blind spot for many leaders in terms of normalising diversity through leading with a multicultural lens, addressing bias and blinders, as well as other taboo topics, such as toxic behaviours in the workplace.

It doesn't matter where you are in terms of geography, or where you are along your D&I journey this is the tool you need. It is not a book you read, it is a highly-valuable instruction manual. Read it and run the play. You need to reprioritise diversity now because the writing is on the wall across all industries and sectors. The rules of the game have changed and Hephzi is giving you the playbook to get us all to the championships.

Dee C Marshall, CEO, Diverse & Engaged, USA, high-profile, global influencer, multi-award-winning business owner and thought leader, focusing on equity, diversity and inclusion across all industry sectors

ABOUT
THE AUTHOR

Hephzi Pemberton is a UK business founder and advisor, who believes in the power of good business to transform society. After completing an undergraduate degree at Oxford University, Hephzi began her career in Investment Banking at Lehman Brothers. In 2009, she co-founded Kea Consultants, a financial headhunting firm that specialises in investment and high-growth organisations, which she quickly grew into a profitable and sustainable business.

In 2018, Hephzi founded Equality Group, an Inclusion and Diversity specialist business focused on the Finance and Technology industry. Equality Group helps companies to diversify their teams, using their executive search service, and creates a more inclusive culture with their consulting and education services. Equality Group has partnered with many leaders in sustainable investing, such as Generation Investment Management, and Private Equity and Venture Capital firms who are committed to being leaders in inclusion and diversity.

Hephzi has been angel investing since 2010 and has invested in technology start-ups across AI, Logistics, Health and Beauty, E-Commerce and Education. She has also advised a number of businesses on their hiring practices, board composition, compensation structure, strategic and fundraising plans.

Alongside her commercial experience, Hephzi has founded a social enterprise called Kiteka, empowering female micro entrepreneurs in Uganda to access digital opportunities through mobile technology. Hephzi has sat on the board of trustees for three other charities focused on youth employment, homelessness and community development.

CONTENTS LIST

|

"The leaders and firms that embrace and embed inclusion and diversity into their business will increase their long-term value.

They will innovate and adapt more rapidly.

They will have a workplace culture that talent seeks out and stays with.

They will reach a wider set of stakeholders, who will feel valued and understood.

They know that to achieve all these benefits you have to take inclusion and diversity seriously."

|

CHAPTER 1
THE TIME HAS COME
WHY INCLUSION MATTERS

"The moment we decide to fulfil something, we can do anything."
Greta Thunberg

Emerging Events

The time has arrived for inclusion. The year 2020 has accelerated our collective awareness of what happens when we exclude whole sections of our society. It has been impossible to ignore the cost of exclusion because of several major issues that emerged, including: the murder of George Floyd in May; Black Lives Matter; and the deep inequalities highlighted by Covid-19. Nor were these events limited solely to civil society. They immediately impacted the private sector with rapid accountability demanded of corporate institutions and leaders.

Suddenly boards and management teams were being asked what they were doing about gender balance and racial justice. Many were deeply underprepared. According to research from Equality Group in March 2021, there were more FTSE 100 CEOs called Andy and Steve, than there were women or ethnic minorities combined.[1] Nor was there a single Black CEO or woman of colour in the list. No wonder boards felt unnerved. For too long inclusion and diversity has sat in the realm of human resources or grassroot employee initiatives. At many firms, it may have only taken the form of a women's network. It was not being discussed regularly at board meetings, with the most senior company stakeholders, as a core part of the business strategy. It was not being considered an area of potential company risk or weakness and equally, a strength and opportunity. However, the issue of inclusion and diversity can no longer be ignored. It is here to stay.

"In March 2021, there were more FTSE 100 CEOs called Andy and Steve, than there were women or ethnic minorities combined."

Long-Term Value

The leaders and firms that embrace and embed inclusion and diversity into their business will increase their long-term value. They will innovate and adapt more rapidly. They will have a workplace culture that talent seeks out and stays with. They will reach a wider set of stakeholders, who will feel valued and understood. They know that to achieve all these benefits you have to take inclusion and diversity seriously.

There is substantial research to show that diversity brings many advantages to an organisation, including: stronger governance; better problem-solving abilities; and increased creativity and profitability.[2] Employees with diverse backgrounds bring a wider range of perspectives, ideas and experiences. They help to create organisations that are resilient and effective, and which outperform organisations that do not invest in diversity.

McKinsey's global study of more than 1,000 large companies found that companies in the top quartile for gender diversity on executive teams were 25 percent more likely to have above-average profitability than companies in the fourth quartile. For ethnic and cultural diversity, top-quartile companies outperformed those in the fourth by 36 percent.

A Boston Consulting Group study found that companies with more diverse management teams have 19 percent higher revenues due to innovation.[3] This finding is significant for tech companies, start-ups and industries where innovation is the key to growth. It shows that diversity is not only a metric to be strived for, it is actually an integral part of a successful revenue-generating business.

Toxic Cultures
The importance of diversity and inclusion in business is not a new one. On the eve of the 2008 global financial crisis, a toxic work culture and a lack of diversity at senior decision-making levels were all cited as reasons for the Lehman Brothers crash. As an analyst at the bank, I saw first-hand how rapidly the culture deteriorated into one of suspicion, sharp elbows and presenteeism before the bankruptcy. As the markets became increasingly volatile and the redundancy rounds ever more frequent, the fault lines in the culture were painfully apparent. I can remember walking into the office on a number of occasions and seeing desks that were once occupied suddenly empty.

Nobody knew what was happening and there was very little communication from senior leadership at the time. Some people said that the bank would never have failed if it had been Lehman Sisters, instead of Lehman Brothers running the bank.[4] This is not true. A group of White women lack diversity exactly as much as a group of White men. Any homogenous group is going to make more mistakes, poorer decisions and fall victim to groupthink.[5] However, having a few more Lehman sisters in the boardroom at the time could have helped manage the fallout better.

Unfortunately, poor management continues to fuel toxic workplace cultures, with bullying especially rife. A third of UK employees surveyed in 2019 by Equality Group said they disliked their work because of how they were managed and two thirds reported quitting a job because they had a bad boss. Polling by Gallup in 2017 showed that only a third of American workers feel actively "involved in, enthusiastic about and committed to their work and workplace."

Despite a focus on raising engagement to boost productivity, this figure has barely improved in 20 years. Globally, the wasted potential is starker: evidence reveals that fewer than one in six employees are engaged.[6] With reviews of most working environments a few clicks away on sites such as Glassdoor, businesses cannot afford to sweep a toxic culture under the rug. As business leaders, it is essential that we learn how to create inclusive cultures and workplaces.

New Leaders Create Diverse Coalitions

In the early 2020 Covid-19 crisis, we saw remarkable results from female national leaders who quickly built diverse coalition partners to manage the crisis. Some of these diverse coalitions are managing to almost halve the number of deaths in their countries compared to their less diverse counterparts.[7] They did this through a combination of greater collaboration, emotional intelligence, effective communication and shrewd risk management. The popular belief that women are more risk-averse has been shown to depend more on the type of risk involved. Many female leaders tend to take a more interpersonal and collaborative approach to problem-solving than their male counterparts, ensuring that they take more people with them once a decision is made.

Truly effective teamwork requires an inclusive corporate culture. People work best when they feel at ease to be themselves and feel valued. Increasing engagement gives employees a stake in the company's purpose, promoting professional and personal growth that reduces staff turnover. These sorts of shifts do not happen by chance. Institutional change needs support from the top, with improved communication, continuous training and well-managed monitoring, which we will explore in more detail later in this playbook.

The Order of The Diversity Playbook

The Diversity Playbook is written as a structured guide to embedding inclusion, diversity and equity across an entire business. The chapters are ordered in the sequence of recommended application, which has been developed through my own work as a consultant, advisor and entrepreneur in this field. Chapters 2 and 3 focus on the importance of leadership and setting the tone from the top. Without this much of the recommended work in later chapters will flounder. Chapter 4 unpacks diversity and inclusion data management and measurement. Chapter 5 explains how to hire more inclusively, outlining several scientifically-grounded techniques and tools to help debias the process. Chapters 6 and 7 explore the most robust inclusion and diversity initiatives and how to effectively incentivise for the desired outcomes. Chapters 8 and 9 discuss how to design the optimal infrastructure and policies to attract, retain and develop your diverse teams. The final chapter widens the lens from inclusion and diversity to the broader theme of social sustainability with a call to action for business leaders globally.

Playbook Chapter Exercises
To create positive organisational and societal change, we need every individual to embrace this process within themselves. As the cultural anthropologist, Margaret Mead, has famously said "never doubt that a small group of thoughtful, committed citizens can change the world; indeed, it's the only thing that ever has." All any business needs is a handful of engaged people who are committed to being the change they want to see. At the end of each chapter in the playbook, there is an interactive exercise for you to personally explore your development journey. Accompanying each exercise is an image of inspirational people who have worked for greater equality and justice throughout history.

This is an invitation for you to reflect on what you have read in this chapter. Once you have considered the first set of questions, as below, I invite you to turn your reflection into action. One of the ways to effectively turn a thought into a deed is to write down your intention to do it. Make a note of your reflective thoughts and your one commitment to action in whatever medium works best for you. You can write it down in your journal; take a note on your telephone; or record a voice-note. The most important factor is to get it down on the page, paper or digital. One step better would be to send it to someone and ask them to follow-up with you, as an accountability check of how you are getting on in a few day's time.

POSITIVE COMMITMENT
EXERCISE

Greta Thunberg is a Swedish environmental activist who is internationally known for challenging world leaders to take immediate action against climate change. In this image, she is speaking at a climate conference in Rome in 2019.

REFLECT

Remember a time when either yourself,
or someone you deeply loved felt excluded.

What did that feel like?

How did that change who you are?

What have you done about it since?

ACT

One way that we can change the negative cycle of exclusion, is to make a positive commitment to become more inclusive. Examples could include educating yourself on an area of diversity you are less familiar with, such as anti-racism, disability or neurodiversity. Another area is reflecting on your communication style with others, and how much space you make for diverse perspectives and voices in your decision making.

Reach out and tell someone you trust and respect that you are making this commitment.

If you cannot think of someone to connect with in this way, please consider joining the Equality Career Lab group on LinkedIn for support and encouragement on the journey.

Growth Mindset

As you travel the path of inclusion, it is helpful to adopt a growth mindset. For those people less familiar with the work of Stanford Professor of Psychology, Carol Dweck, a growth mindset is having the belief that everyone, including yourself has the capacity to learn and improve over time. A growth mindset allows yourself and other people to get things wrong, to learn from your mistakes and to incrementally improve. It is not a belief that everyone can achieve the same level of proficiency, but it does mean everyone can improve their own level of proficiency. The opposite of a growth mindset is a fixed mindset, which is a belief that what you are born with is what you are stuck with. That if you are born White and male, then you can never understand what it might be like to be Black and female. With a growth mindset, you are inviting yourself to try to understand a little bit more about the Black female experience, for example. You will never fully understand it as well as actually being Black and female, but you will get that bit closer to being able to understand a different perspective and lived experience.

Your Choice

We can all choose to adopt a growth mindset to inclusion and diversity. The process of evolving and improving over time allows us to become more inclusive. If we have walked that path ourselves, then we will allow other people to do so and even inspire others to do so. For anyone in the business world, it has become essential that you consider how to become more inclusive. This is because inclusion and diversity, like climate change, are not to be ignored. They will shape the way businesses evolve and remain competitive, or flatline and fade into extinction, as Lehman Brothers did.

●

THOUGHTS

CHAPTER 2
LEAD AND LEARN
INCLUSIVE LEADERSHIP

"Reach in for the stars; go within yourself and search for the hidden, latent, buried and unknown talents that you can bring out and use to lighten, brighten the darkness or minimise the setbacks of people around you."

Dr Christiana Ayoka Mary Thorpe

When it comes to leading, we must always keep developing. Leaders who want to see inclusion and diversity progress in their organisation understand that the process starts with them. For example, when Satya Nadella came into his role as CEO of Microsoft in 2014, he was determined to enhance the organisation with a culture of learning, especially in the areas are of inclusion and innovation. The encouragement he gave to the company was to "always keep learning. You stop doing useful things if you don't learn." Too often the inclusion and diversity agendas are limited to the HR departments of companies, rather than the strategic growth and innovation domains where they also belong. The C-suite and boards who take personal ownership of inclusion and diversity are the ones who see real and tangible progress made in their business. Unfortunately, it often takes something going wrong, such as a sexual harassment lawsuit, or negative press coverage, before the need for change is acknowledged. The reputational, financial and personal risks of homogeneity and exclusion are issues that smart leaders take seriously and anticipate. They also see the multiple business opportunities that an inclusion and diversity lens can bring to their business. Leaders set the tone for other people to follow. If you can be a more authentic leader, you will naturally create a more inclusive business that can optimise for diversity.

Representative Leadership

When it comes to leadership: how you lead is as important as who is leading. Progress on inclusion and diversity can be made when the leader at the top becomes more inclusive, even if they are from a dominant group. Much has been made about who is leading an organisation, given the continued under-representation of women and ethnic minorities at the top.

The need for representative leadership that reflects the communities, consumers and stakeholders in our society has never been greater. However, representation doesn't necessarily lead to inclusion. From recent research at Equality Group on stereotypes in leadership they found that a quarter of UK women felt that female bosses express more gender bias towards women than male managers.[8] This counterintuitive trend has also been shown in research by Dolly Chugh at NYU Stern. Women, as a whole, show stronger implicit gender bias than men and Black Americans are as likely to show pro-White implicit race bias as pro-Black implicit race bias.[9] However, it is worth keeping in mind that White people very reliably show pro-White implicit bias, while Black people are more even on their results – being about as likely to show pro-White as pro-Black bias.

Bias and Balance

One of the reasons for greater gender or racial bias in certain groups is the pressure to assimilate to the dominant cultural narrative. Equality Group research shows that a fifth of UK women feel they have to present themselves in more stereotypically masculine ways to succeed in their jobs. To be accepted in the traditionally masculine world of work, women not only have to play by the rules of the game, they have to excel at the game. Yet, this pressure on women to cultivate traditionally masculine qualities while remaining inherently female is a double standard with unexpected benefits. It has taught female leaders to be more resourceful, notes Bobbi

Thomason at the Pepperdine Graziadio Business School. Aware of facing greater scrutiny, women are more likely to consult a wider network when making decisions while ensuring they are backed up by evidence. As women in business have learnt how to be more like men, perhaps we need more men in business to learn how to be more like women. A combination of the best of masculine and feminine traits is one that takes us closer to an inclusive form of leadership.

Inclusive Leadership Traits

What are the core characteristics of inclusive leadership? There are many different frameworks. The models used by some companies list twenty-plus behaviours.[10] The most effective are memorable and meaningful enough to be implemented daily. As a starting point, let's explore six core characteristics of inclusive leaders. These are outlined below, but can be adapted for the values and language of any organisation.

1) **Positive commitment;** taking personal responsibility for change, based on the business case for diversity and inclusion and a deeply rooted sense of fairness.
2) **Courage and humility;** fearlessly challenging attitudes and practices that yield homogeneity, while acknowledging personal limits and seeking input from other people.
3) **Awareness of bias;** continually making an effort to identify blind spots and ingrained assumptions that get in the way of objective decision-making.
4) **Curiosity and active listening;** institutionalising open-mindedness by listening carefully to different perspectives so all employees feel valued and respected.
5) **Emotional and cultural intelligence;** developing enough self-awareness to respond with sensitivity to different personalities and cultural contexts.
6) **Collaborative and generous;** understanding that teams work best when people feel empowered to share their opinions, while encouraging diverse perspectives.

At Microsoft, Satya Nadella, emphasised the qualities of emotional intelligence and active listening. These are two traits that might traditionally have been referred to as feminine qualities. Early on in his leadership journey, Satya identified them as key competitive advantages. One of the experiences that he believes contributed more than anything to strengthening his sense of empathy was when he became a parent. His first child, born when Satya and his wife were 25 and 29 years old respectively, suffers from Cerebral palsy which prevents him from speaking and moving his limbs. Nadella has said that; "At first, I did nothing but ask myself; Why did this happen to me?, I began to understand that absolutely nothing had happened to me. In reality this thing had happened to my son and for me it was time to see life through his eyes and to do what I was supposed to, as a parent and a father".[11] This lesson in greater empathy at home, then translated further into his work and became a priority in business for him every day.

Culture Makers

While many leaders think culture is important, most of them are not prioritizing it. According to a 2018 Accenture study only 21 percent of leaders identify culture as a top priority and only 23 percent have set a related target or goal.[12] This is despite employees placing a high amount of value on the ability to be their true and authentic selves while at work. Culture makers are advocates. They are much more likely to have spoken out on a range of issues, including gender equality (52 percent versus 35 percent of all leaders) and sexual harassment/discrimination (51 percent versus 30 percent). They hold themselves accountable, leading organisations that are 1.8x more likely to have publicly announced a target to get more women into the workforce. And they model being the same person both inside and outside of work. At least 85 percent believe that senior leaders who talk openly about personal hardships and challenges are stronger leaders. Notably, they lead organisations that are growing more than twice as fast as those of their peers. In fact, they report their sales are 2.2x higher and their profits are 3.2x higher.

Prejudice

Developing as an inclusive leader is like learning any topic that requires skill. The more you know, the more you appreciate what you don't know. At the same time, it requires a degree of skill in this area to know what you have to develop. This is known as the Dunning-Kruger Effect, which suggests that when we don't know something, we aren't aware of our own lack of knowledge. This is particularly true about the topic of egalitarianism and how racist or sexist you are as an individual. When this test was completed by Equality Group's head of research, Dr Keon West, it showed that most people overestimate how egalitarian they actually are, compared to an external measure.

The results from this study and many others are a humbling reminder of the work we all have to do to become more inclusive, whether we are leading companies or not.

PREJUDICED AND UNAWARE OF IT
EVIDENCE FOR THE DUNNING-KRUGER MODEL IN THE DOMAINS OF RACISM AND SEXISM

Dr Keon West (keon.west@gold.ac.uk), **Dr Asia A Eaton** (aeaton@fiu.edu)

Often, individuals who are incompetent are also unaware of their incompetence, because they lack the skills needed to recognise (in)competence. This is called the Dunning-Kruger effect.

Two studies on racism (N=148) and sexism (n=159) tested whether egalitarianism also functioned as a skill and whether the Dunning-Kruger effect also applied in this domain.

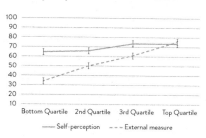

Egalitarianism:
Self-perception **vs.** External Measure

— Self-perception   - - - External measure

In both studies, as hypothesised, the least egalitarian (i.e., most prejudiced) participants were also the ones who most strongly overestimated their own egalitaranism, making them both prejudiced and unaware of their prejudice.

West, K., & Eaton, A.A. (2019). Prejudiced and unaware of it: Evidence for the Dunning-Kruger model in the domains of racism and sexism. *Personality and Individual Differences*, DOI: https//doi.org/10.1016/j.paid.2019.03.047.

Develop Your Competency

One of the ways to better understand leadership abilities and areas for development is by gathering and receiving 360 feedback, also known as multi-source or multi-rater feedback. The purpose is to gather information about an individual's performance from a variety of people with whom the individual interacts on a regular basis. This process ideally encompasses people the individual works with, such as: direct reports; peers; and management, as well as people that they work for, including: clients; and customers. This holistic insight into the way someone currently leads, measured against the leadership dimensions above or similar criteria is a helpful framework for becoming more inclusive. Making it an annual review process can bring about real change and accountability. Working with a coach is another way to gain greater insights and progress inclusive leadership traits.

Another helpful tool for developing and deepening your inclusive leadership abilities is to complete an audit of your inner circle, which is defined as the top five people in your life who you trust and confide in. If there was something going wrong at home or at work, who do you call? Avoid your immediate family or intimate partner in this list. Close friends who you also talk to about work can be featured. Once you have made the list, complete a number of columns with different diversity demographics that are important to you and your organisation. The table below gives an outline example of what this looks like.

Your Inner Circle Audit

Names	Gender (F)	Ethnicity	Sexuality - LGBT+	Socio-economic	Disability	Any other dimension
Person 1	●	●		●		
Person 2	●		●	●		
Person 3	●					
Person 4				●		
Person 5	●			●		

Once you have completed the table, note where you have the most gaps. When I first completed this, I was painfully aware of my affinity bias, which is a preference for people who are most similar to you. My table was filled primarily with White, educated women in their mid-thirties. I had work to do on gender, age, disability and racial equality. The first action to take is to expand your network of friends and advisors. There are many options for network expansion now with all the digital networks available to us, as well as proactive reaching out to individuals who you know have a different background and perspective to you. Two years after completing this work myself, the Equality Group advisory board took shape. It was built with the knowledge that diverse boards make better decisions and the desire to have an inner circle that looked and thought very differently to me.

|

"Prioritise learning, lead by example
and build diverse teams."

|

INCLUSIVE LEADERSHIP
EXERCISE

Martin Luther King Jr. was an African American Baptist minister and activist who became the most visible spokesperson and leader in the American civil rights movement from 1955 until his assassination in 1968. King advanced civil rights through nonviolence and civil disobedience, inspired by his Christian beliefs and the nonviolent activism of Mahatma Gandhi.

|

REFLECT

Of the leadership traits listed above, which one
would you most like to develop in the next month?

Why is this one particularly important to you?

What would developing this trait look like
in your work and in your relationships?

ACT

Commit to the leadership trait development process by:
a) writing it down;
b) giving yourself a score out of 5 of where you are now
and where you would like to be in a month's time; and
c) telling someone in your inner circle that you will be working
on this for the next month.

|

Show The Way

As leaders, we have a responsibility to set an inclusive example that our teams can follow. It is also an example that other leaders will want to follow. That has happened to Satya Nadella, time and time again. Recently, the Volkswagen CEO Herbert Diess called him to ask for advice about managing change. The change was across the entire industry – from hardware and a focus on car owners – to a software-led, mobility-first business model. All of this while trying to rebuild an organisational culture recovering from the company's global Dieselgate scandal in 2015. Satya's main advice to Herbert centred on the development work he had achieved as an inclusive leader. Prioritising learning, leading by example, and building diverse teams were at the heart of his message. They are the core ingredients for transforming good leaders into inclusive leaders. With more leaders like Satya, more learners like Herbert and more readers like you, we will start to see a significant shift towards inclusion across industries.

THOUGHTS

CHAPTER 3
COMMUNICATION IS KEY
WELCOME WORDS

"It's important for us to pause for a moment and make sure that we are talking with each other in a way that heals, not a way that wounds.."
Barack Obama

Our words have the power to transform. They have the power to heal. They have the power to welcome. Thoughtfully chosen and carefully communicated, they can signal to every stakeholder what really matters. An absence of mindful communication is a dangerous void in organisations. The fear of making a mistake or of being criticised often prevents leaders from speaking up on the topic of inclusion and diversity.

However, the necessary vulnerability that comes from talking about our common humanity and the biases within our society and systems is part of the learning needed to be an inclusive leader. When we speak about these topics, we learn more about them, we engage in dialogue, we connect and create the environment for other peoples to thrive. This is not a clean process. It is messy. It requires courage, humility, openness and curiosity. All qualities of an inclusive leader. When you are committed to the process of inclusion, then you are wise to reflect on and use words that demonstrate your values.

Know Your Destination
The first step in any journey is figuring out where you want to go. However, this may be less straightforward than it sounds. Often the same goal can be framed in different ways: you can focus on the

behaviours you want to encourage, such as being more inclusive; or on those you want to prevent, such as the risk of harassment.[13] A wealth of psychological research has shown that a focus on positives, on the outcome you want to happen, typically leads to better results. Focusing on prevention, on the other hand, often makes matters worse regardless of the intention behind it.[14] For example, even when individuals are actively trying to reduce their prejudice and promote egalitarian values, a focus on preventing prejudiced behaviours, rather than promoting inclusion, tends to work against them and ends up increasing prejudice.[15]

Language Differences

How often have you referred to the chairman or the salesman, rather than the chair or the salesperson at work? It may seem a trivial, irrelevant difference, but research shows that the use of gender-specific language significantly alters our sense of who belongs in a particular position. Women who hear male-specific language during an interview – even something as subtle as using the pronoun 'he' exclusively when discussing the role – feel less belonging, less identification with the job, and less motivation to do it well.[16]

A subtle shift to gender-inclusive language flips all those effects and creates more belonging, more identification, and more motivation. In a similar vein, research by academics Jane Stout and Nilanjana Dasgupta in 2011 showed that using gender-inclusive language signals more positive attitudes toward transgender and gender nonconforming individuals.[17] There are many other benefits to using inclusive pronouns as well, including a reduction in stereotypes and discrimination.[18] This is a very small linguistic change with very large benefits.

One of the most challenging aspects of language is how rapidly it evolves. Indeed, universally agreed language about issues relating to race are almost non-existent. Even the most frequently used words in any discussion on ethnicity can easily cause confusion and at worst controversy and hostility. It is essential to achieve a degree of shared understanding, particularly when using the most common terms.

For example, given the changing demographic trends in the US, the word 'minority' no longer accurately reflects the four-primary racial/ethnic groups. The terms 'emerging majority' and 'people of colour' have become popular substitutes for this grouping term. The term BAME – Black, Asian and Minority Ethnic – has long been used in the UK to define people from an ethnic minority. In the UK, that is approximately 13 percent of the population. However, it has its limitations and many would prefer that the term was no longer used given that it masks the lived experiences of individual groups.

Labels

Using a term like BAME, allows the topic to be raised, while not necessarily acknowledging the level of nuance necessary to have meaningful conversations about race and ethnicity in the workplace. It gives permission to glaze over the variety of specific issues different ethnic groups might face. Grouping a wide range of ethnic minorities together under a single 'non-White' grouping is a starting point, but not the end point. At the same time, labels such as BAME and LGBTQ+ allow disparate groups, bound together by similar, though not identical, experiences to collectively act and to be represented in greater numbers. Acknowledging the limitations of labels when using them helps to demonstrate an awareness of the power and the poverty of words.

Beyond the individual groupings within many of the diversity labels are the overlapping layers of identity within those groupings. The term 'intersectionality' has grown in usage during recent years. It describes the combination of different demographic identities that each of us have.

For example, I am a White, cis-gender, university educated, English woman.[19] In this description, I have listed four categories of diversity that I identify with. How I feel about each of them will depend on many factors, including the reception in society and at work. The reality is that I experience a huge amount of privilege in belonging to these groups. The term privilege is used here to describe the benefits granted to members of a specific group solely by being members of that group. Privilege is not earned and it is usually not noticed, nor desired, by those who enjoy its benefits. However, what it does mean is that my life has had significantly fewer barriers than if I was a Black woman who identified as transgender, had never attended university and lived in a country that outlawed her gender identity.

"Put down your armour; be prepared to be wrong; use the words that welcome; and listen more than you speak."

Connect With Your Audience

Developing an understanding of the key terminology and topics on diversity and inclusion is critical to inclusive leadership. A recent example of effective connection with a critical audience comes from Joe Biden's campaign to connect directly with Black American voters through "Lift Every Voice".[20] This plan outlined critical issues that matter to Black Americans, such as the Black-White income gap, expanding educational opportunities, investing $70 billion in H.B.C.U.s and reimagining the criminal justice system and policing. Mr. Biden's selection of Vice President-elect Kamala Harris, the first Black woman on a major party ticket, was taken as a symbolic affirmation of these commitments. Former President Barack Obama, the country's first Black president, had to assure White America he would be a president for all races. But Mr. Biden repeatedly asserted that Black communities would get special attention in his administration.

It is essential that leaders are proactive, like Joe Biden, about updating their language and ensuring they know the words that will connect their communities, rather than divide them. As times have changed and language has evolved, many leaders have fallen behind with their understanding and fluency in the language of inclusion. Given the knowledge gap that exists, inclusion education is one of the cornerstones of the work business leaders need to do. They need to be able to know what they need and how to communicate effectively.

Voice Your Truth

There are times when modesty is an important value, but this is not one of them. When you value inclusion and diversity, you need to vocalise it. A survey the Equality Group conducted in 2019 of more than 2,000 UK professionals showed that ethnic minorities are less likely to believe that their organisation takes issues of inclusion and diversity seriously rather than it being only a tokenistic exercise.[21] Making it clear where you stand on the topic, before you have to be asked or interviewed about it is advisable. There are studies showing that a clear statement of positivity about diversity makes underrepresented groups perform better at a variety of tasks, since they are not using up cognitive resources trying to figure out where they stand.[22]

There are other benefits as well. Even in the most well-meaning, diverse, and inclusive companies, mistakes will sometimes occur, even if by accident. And even when everything is going relatively well, sometimes ambiguous or unclear messages can cause offence. The good news is that the right environment can help everyone feel better about these instances and respond better to them. The more upfront you are about your inclusion and diversity values, the more likely your employees are to see ambiguous instances in a favourable way.

If an unfortunate incident has occurred, then they will respond more sympathetically if you have been clear about your inclusive values.[23] One of the most important aspects of remote working is the need for increased communication, which gives you many opportunities to come back to your inclusive values and practices as an organisation. There is no reason to hold it in. When you value inclusion and diversity, let people know. Your workplace will benefit from your openness.

VISIBLE DIVERSITY
EXERCISE

US President Barack Obama with the first lady Michelle Obama next to him gives a speech from the East Room of the White House June 29, 2009 in Washington, DC. The words of Michelle Obama and Barack Obama have been hailed as inspiring, welcoming and healing for many around the world.

REFLECT
How visible is your support of inclusion and diversity
on your website, your company materials, your social media
and in your meetings?

ACT
How could you make it more visible today?

What do you want to promote more of in your business?

If you are on social media, what could you post to make clear
your support and commitment to inclusion and diversity?

A Positive Statement

The work of Brene Brown, the research professor at the University of Houston, who has spent most of her career studying shame, guilt, vulnerability and courage offers powerful advice for leaders. She said: "You can't be brave if you're tapping out of hard conversations about painful, hard topics. That's what it means to lead".[24]

Brown demonstrated in her book *Daring Greatly* that to become better leaders we not only need to embrace the pain and discomfort of difficult subjects, but we also need to put down the defensive emotional armour that we often carry into those arenas. The topic of inclusion and diversity raises several uncomfortable feelings and can trigger painful emotions and reactions. As you venture further into this territory, it is important to remember to put down your armour; be prepared to be wrong; use the words that welcome; and listen more than you speak.

THOUGHTS

CHAPTER 4
DATA MATTERS
BENEFITS FOR
COMPLIANT COMPANIES

"What gets measured, gets managed."
Peter Drucker

If words are the welcome, then data sets the agenda. As with any area of business management, what is measured, is managed. You never set out to grow a division of your business without sourcing key business data to inform your planning. The same is true with inclusion and diversity. If you understand that this is a critical driver of strategic growth, then you will approach it with the same rigour and thoughtfulness. However, there are challenges when it comes to what data you should gather and how to go about the data collection in a sensitive and legal manner. Many firms fear what measuring their inclusion and diversity data will tell them. Others are worried about the legality and consequences of disclosure. But knowing where you stand is better than not knowing at all. We are living in a time where the risk of not measuring the data far outweighs the fear of collecting it and what it may reveal.

Information Power
It is important to appreciate that social sustainability data is an emerging area. There are very few companies that have been collecting and managing inclusion and diversity numbers for more than a decade. Many companies have not even begun the journey. The issue therefore, ranges from a total lack of information at some firms, to the inconsistency, the infrequency and the lack of transparency at

others. In the UK, the concept of diversity data was put squarely on the agenda by mandatory gender pay gap reporting.

The new legislation, introduced in 2017, targeted companies with 250 or more employees and covered 34 percent of the UK workforce. However, in 2020 the government decided to pause the reporting requirement due to the Covid pandemic. It was the only company reporting requirement deferred in that year. An unfortunate case in point of the inconsistency and infrequency that can often accompany social sustainability data. However, the tide is turning, and it is only a matter of time before the race pay gap will be introduced, alongside gender pay gap reporting.

Richer Data and Rewards

Companies who anticipate and embrace inclusion and diversity data now will see huge benefits. This will mean capturing more than the basics of gender diversity, such as the gender pay gap or the number of women on boards. This is not to say that this isn't a good place to start. If you work for a firm that doesn't even have this data captured or published, then either measure it, or ask for it. However, it is not the gold standard. Measuring the number of women on boards as the main indicator of inclusion and diversity at a company is as limited as sourcing data from one competitor's product to develop your entire pricing strategy. Diversity data needs to be broader and richer than gender ratios at the most senior level of a company. The braver companies will be about asking their employees for diversity and inclusion data, the better the quality of the data and the decisions that are made as a result.

"Companies who lead on social sustainability data measurement and management are reaping multiple benefits."

Balance and Breadth

An additional risk that emerges from being too reliant on one or two individual diversity and inclusion metrics can be found in "Goodhart's Law". This concept is named after British economist Charles Goodhart, who advanced the idea in a 1975 article on monetary policy in the UK, when he wrote that "any observed statistical regularity will tend to collapse once pressure is placed upon it for control purposes."[25] The anthropologist Marilyn Strathern later recognised that this law could apply in domains beyond economics. She summed up Goodhart's Law as: "when a measure becomes a target, it ceases to be a good measure."[26]

Part of the reason for this paradoxical law is that a single data point can be too easily manipulated. When data is collected, people will refine their behaviors to optimise for that data point, which makes it a less valuable measure than before. An example of this from my consulting experience was with an investment firm claiming a significant increase in female board representation over the past 12 months. The reality was that they had managed to find one female board member and persuaded her to sit on four of their boards. This is an increase in the key metric, but not to the extent that one would imagine from the headline number. One of the ways to mitigate this risk is to have a broad and robust set of metrics across diversity, equity and inclusion that reduces the ability or temptation to massage a single data point.

A Gender Equality Approach

Georgi Ganev, the CEO of Kinnevik, a Swedish Investment Company, demonstrated this in 2018 when he met with his board to discuss how the firm could progress their gender equality. Equality Group was mandated to help develop the inclusion and diversity strategy and roadmap, informed with relevant data collection and analysis. Ahead of the data gathering exercise, Georgi communicated the importance of the topic to the entire organisation. Everyone at the firm, across offices, levels and functions was invited to participate in the process. This made it an inclusive exercise from the start. The data gathering work could then begin. It was conducted by an audit through a quantitative survey, and qualitative one-on-one interviews. Inviting a third party to gather the data, analyse and present it back to the firm, helped to ensure that five key principles were maintained during the process.

1. Objectivity
2. Sensitivity
3. Anonymity
4. Confidentiality
5. Legality

Upholding these five principles are essential to incorporate at every stage of inclusion and diversity data gathering and analysis. Where these are not adhered to, there are serious risks ranging from employee resentment to legal action. That is why having the right expertise on your team, who adhere to these principles is imperative and will set you up for success.

Best Practice
Inclusion and diversity data collection needs to focus on best practice across the market, which includes conducting the following methodology.

- Start the process as early in the company's life as possible; the smaller, the better.
- Collect external data to allow for industry benchmarks.
- Never reinvent the wheel. Use insights and tools from external resources and experts.
- Identify and recruit key stakeholders across the organisation.
- Build a short, concise survey where each question matches up to a goal or objective.
- Communicate and set expectations upfront with all employees; be transparent with the intentions and timely with the process and results. Employees need to understand the Why behind collecting the data.

The gold standard for diversity data is intersectional in nature. This means considering the full range of demographic diversity factors that could be captured and analysed. In the diagram below, you can see the spectrum of demographic and cognitive diversity areas to consider in data gathering exercises.

A BROADER SPECTRUM

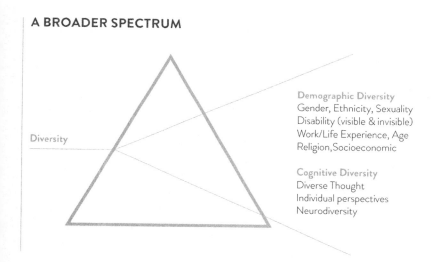

Diversity

Demographic Diversity
Gender, Ethnicity, Sexuality
Disability (visible & invisible)
Work/Life Experience, Age
Religion, Socioeconomic

Cognitive Diversity
Diverse Thought
Individual perspectives
Neurodiversity

Segment Engagement Data

Many organisations conduct employee engagement surveys, but most neglect to segment the data they collect by criteria, including: gender; ethnicity; generation; geography; tenure; and role in the organisation. By only looking at the total numbers, employers miss out on opportunities to identify issues among smaller groups that could be leading to attrition. In 2015, for example, women constituted 52 percent of the new associate class at global law firm Baker McKenzie, but only 23 percent of the firm's 1,510 partners.[27] Karen Brown who was the Director of Diversity and Inclusion at the time, found that the underlying cause was the firm's women associates didn't want to be partners nearly as much as their male counterparts. In a follow-up survey they found out the reasons for this. It was not a lack of overall career ambition. It came down to four things that they needed in the firm, including: more flexibility around working location and hours; better access to high-profile engagements; greater commitment to the firm's diversity targets; and more women role models. Those four aspects became the basis for an action plan that included, for example, a firm-wide flexible work program that promoted remote working. By 2018, the percentage of women promoted to partner had risen to 40, up from 26 in 2015.

Dig Deeper
In the quest for high-quality diversity data, addressing topics within intersectionality becomes critically important. In short, different groups must be recognised to have potentially differing needs and drivers to participate in a quest for wider inclusion and diversity. The consultancy Bain & Company have shown the vast differences that can emerge within culture survey data when an intersectional approach is applied. For example, in the Net Promoter Score (NPS) measuring employee engagement across FTSE 100 companies 2018, in the figure below, you can see the difference between a simple gender analysis and an intersectional analysis.

EMPLOYEE NET PROMOTER SCORE®

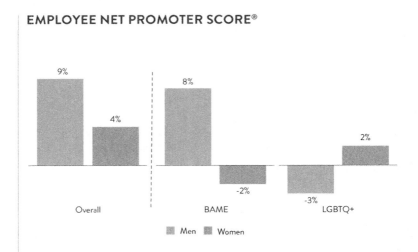

Notes: Net Promoter®, Net Promoter System®, Net Promoter Score® and NPS® are registered trademarks
of Bain & Company, Inc., Fred Reicheld and Satmetrix Systems, Inc.
BAME stands for black, Asian and minority ethnic; LGBTQ+ stands for lesbian, gay, bisexual, transgender, queer, plus
Source: Bain & Company Diversity and Inclusiob in the workplace, 2018 (n=4,521, weighted to reflect UK and Ireland market

In the graph above, when the gender split data was further broken down further by BAME and LGBTQ+, it showed the significantly lower NPS of BAME women and LGBTQ+ men. This level of granularity allows companies to create strategy, policies and processes that specifically address the needs of these communities and engage them in making positive change.

LGBTQ+ is often seen as an icebreaker approach to evaluating inclusion data in corporate culture. One of the reasons for this is because by its very nature addressing the topic of LGBTQ+ rights requires organisations to think in a more nuanced ways about the meaning of gender, sexuality and identity. Where the Gender Lens approach has often taken a heteronormative, cis-gender and binary understanding of diversity, the LGBTQ+ Lens encompasses many more forms of gender expressions, sexual orientations, lifestyle norms and expectations.

Look Beneath the Iceberg
An LGBTQ+ Lens also expands our understanding of invisible diversity factors, which includes many other forms of identity, such as religion, neurodiversity, hidden disabilities and mental health. Despite this, a reasonable pushback is that this could perpetuate a siloed approach to the topic. A diversity-by-diversity analysis risks a potentially damaging competition for resource allocations and management awareness between diversity segments, such as gender versus LGBTQ+. However, it is when LGBTQ+ data is used as a tool to drive inclusion more broadly that it becomes particularly valuable. An understanding of LGBTQ+ encourages employees to feel comfortable and safe being out and authentic at work as their diversity is otherwise invisible.

Sensitive Statistics
Nevertheless, the invisibility of much diversity data remains a challenge. In 2018, a report by Stonewall showed that more than a third of UK employees are not publicly out about their sexuality at work.[28] Equality Group's report a year later showed that almost 40 percent of employees believe their management are under-equipped

to address issues of homophobia at work.[29] These results indicate that there is a still a long way to go in a country that prides itself on values of respect and free speech. Consider how much untapped potential, wealth and prosperity there is from the LGBTQ+ community in a country like Nigeria, where more than half of LGBTQ+ people experience threats to their lives and extreme prejudice and stigmatisation at work.

Not only is diversity data invisible through personal choice, but also through fear of state law. In Europe, there is a common misconception that data protection legislation prohibits the collection of sensitive data revealing racial or ethnic origin or religion. In the EU and across all Member States' laws, equality data collection is permitted as long as the data is provided voluntarily and according to data protection standards. The EU Data Protection Directive stipulates exceptions to prohibition of processing sensitive personal data,

such as data revealing ethnic or racial origin or religion, when:

- express consent is given;
- the State has obligations in the field of employment law;
- for protection of the rights of other people's; or
- for reasons of substantial public interest.

This is why appropriate leadership, communication and expertise are required to ensure effective data management and measurement.

DIVERSITY BENCHMARKING
EXERCISE

*Amelia Earhart was the first female aviator to fly solo across
the Atlantic Ocean in 1928. She set many other records
and wrote best-selling books about her flying experiences.
She was instrumental in the formation of The Ninety-Nines,
an organization for female pilots.*

|

REFLECT

1. How much diversity and inclusion data does your company measure and manage? List all the areas that you are aware of, or have access to.

ACT

2. Evaluate how you rank on inclusion and diversity data through the Equality Group Inclusive Index Score available on request by email: hello@equality.group.

3. Take this data back to your board and senior leadership to collectively reflect on.

|

Business Benefits

There is a significant market opportunity for companies who demonstrate that diversity and inclusion data matters to them. It signals a commitment to and ambition for social sustainability to investors, customers, employees and regulatory bodies alike. In Equality Group's LGBTQ+ Lens research, more than 90 percent of investment professionals cited a lack of consistent and well-understood LGBTQ+ data at the companies they research, to be a ble to underpin a robust investment process.[30] While investors struggle to access this data, they will also struggle to integrate social sustainability into their investment priorities. However, companies who have this data already measured and published are increasingly attracting greater levels of funding. In 2019, global sustainable investments rose by 34 percent year on year to a total of US$30.7 trillion.[31] Companies who lead on social sustainability data measurement and management are reaping multiple benefits.

THOUGHTS

CHAPTER 5
INCLUSIVE HIRING
DEBIASED SYSTEMS

"Erasing all the individual 'rot' in the world
would not lead to equality
until our systems were also debiased."
Dolly Chugh

The traditional recruitment process is riddled with bias. This in turn minimises effective decision making. To ensure we are hiring inclusively and smartly, there are several scientifically-grounded techniques and tools to understand and utilise. Debiasing systems takes courage and effort. There is often an attachment to systems and processes that have been used for a long time. Many of us like to believe that we are an excellent judge of character. In our personal lives this may have served us well. When it comes to hiring talent, individual judgements are potentially dangerous derailers for effective team building. The evidence for increasing diversity, long-term job performance and retention by debiasing the hiring process is striking. If your organisation is serious about building diverse teams, then ensuring an objective and less biased process is essential.

The Bias Barrier
One of the greatest barriers to achieving equal representation in the workforce is bias. A wealth of research in multiple countries has consistently found that bias prevents equal access to employment and leadership opportunities. A significant number of studies have shown entrenched gender bias at work at every stage of the career

journey. Even when other differences are eliminated or controlled, women are offered less pay than men for the same work, offered less informal support when joining organisations, and offered fewer and less desirable leadership positions.[32]

Ethnic Minority Call-Back Rates

In a recent British field experiment covering 3,200 job opportunities, academics found that ethnic minorities got call-back rates that were less than half the rates of White applicants, despite being identically qualified.[33] As shown in the graph below, 24 percent of majority group applicants got a call-back from employers. Despite identical resumes and cover letters, minorities had to send 60 percent more applications in order to receive as many call-backs. Nigerian and Pakistani names received the lowest call-back rates overall.

PREDICTED CALLBACK RATES OF PAKISTANI AND NIGERIAN APPLICANTS COMPARED TO THE MAJORITY GROUP AND ALL OTHER MINORITIES COMBINED

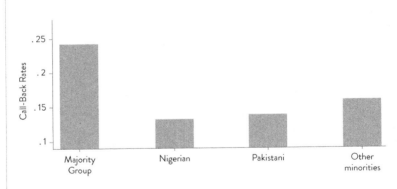

Note: probabilities of receiving a callback estimated from linear probability moels, controlling for religion and generational status of the applicant (2ⁿᵈ vs. 1.5 generation)

Inclusive Role Descriptions

Critical to any hiring decision is a clearly defined and communicated role description. To achieve this focus on the competencies and experiences required to be successful in the role. Avoid having a dream candidate in mind or comparing the ideal person to anyone else in the organisation. This will ensure a more inclusive process and avoid unconscious biases creeping in. There are many competency-based templates available for roles on the internet. It is worth cross-checking your template with other online versions to ensure you have as broad a specification as possible. This will increase your chances of being able to recruit from a wider talent pool. A role description based on core skills and qualities will enable you to develop specific competency-based questions to ask during the interview process, rather than relying on individual judgements.

It is also worth being aware of coded language which can attract, or deter, certain groups of candidates from applying. In terms of gender diversity, research shows that certain masculine-coded phrases and words (for example adjectives including, competitive and determined) reduce the likelihood of women applying to jobs.[34] There are free software programs available to scan role descriptions for gendered words – ensuring that adverts are not actively discouraging applications from certain gender groups. One example is Textio, which helps you remove gender-biased terms from your adverts, or the free version called Gender Decoder. Additionally, it is worth stating in the advert that your company is committed to inclusion and diversity.[35]

"A clear statement about diversity helps underrepresented groups perform better."

When you create a recruitment advert for wider circulation of the role consider a 70/30 approach. This will help increase your chances of attracting diverse talent. The rule states that 70 percent of the advert should describe the company's culture, values and leadership while only 30 percent should focus on the role, assignment and requirements. Company values, culture and the leadership approach are among the most important decision factors for choosing an employer. However, many companies make the mistake of focusing more than 90 percent of the job advert on a long list of requirements needed to apply for the job.

Anonymise the Resume
A focus on specific skills, qualities, and values of candidates, rather than demographic factors, such as the exact university they studied at, helps to level the playing field. As we have seen from the callback rate data, the fact is that people called Latisha and Jamal do not get the same number of call-backs as Emily and Greg. A blind, systematic process for reviewing applications and resumes will help you improve your chances of including the most relevant candidates in your interview pool, including uncovering the hidden gems. This can be done manually and for free, by having someone in your team remove the signifying characteristics (names, pictures, firm, university and school names, and any other identifying demographic traits). Alternatively, you can use software programs, such as Blendoor, which removes irrelevant data from the recruitment process to ensure candidates are hired based on merit. The talent software company, Applied, has developed a program to remove the CV from the hiring process and focuses purely on the skills required for the role.

Standardised Interviews
Although it can be tempting to have an informal and free-flowing discussion with someone you are meeting for the first time, this is highly unlikely to result in an effective hire. Unstructured interviews that lack defined questions and where a candidate's experience and expertise are meant to unfold organically through the conversation are fundamentally bad at predicting job success.[36] On the other hand, structured interviews, where each candidate is asked the same set of defined questions relating to their values and skills, help to minimise bias and focus on the factors that have a direct impact on long-term job performance. Ideally, there is an interview scorecard that grades candidates' responses to each value or skills-based question, on a predetermined scale. At the same time, it is important to remember that creating rapport and connection is an important part

of the interview process. Allowing time for informal conversation and follow-on questions from the core standard set of questions is the best way to balance bias mitigation with relationship building.

"Confirmation bias is where you seek out and pay more attention to information that confirms your initial preconceptions."

In addition to a structured set of questions, it is preferable for interviewers not to know the specifics about how well each candidate scored in other interviews, assessments or tests. This is to avoid introducing confirmation bias to your hiring process. Confirmation bias is where you seek out and pay more attention to information that confirms your initial preconceptions. Often confirmation bias comes in between interview stages, as well as during the interview. When we discuss what we like or didn't like about a candidate with someone else and they agree with us, it can confirm what we thought, without necessarily taking into account all the data available on a candidate before making a decision. As much as possible, individual data points, which are each stage of the interview process, should be assessed and scored separately. This allows for uncorrelated data gathering throughout the interview process and reduces how much confirmation bias can occur.

This simple, 7-step interview assessment process is an objective guide to reduce the chances of making biased decisions based on opinion and gut instincts.

1. Design a clear process, with a diverse panel of interviewers. Minimise the number of formal stages wherever possible.
2. Use competency-based, structured interviews where all candidates are asked the same pre-defined questions, ideally in the same order.
3. Interview separately and avoid group interviews.

4. Allow time for free-flowing conversation and follow-on questions.
5. Bring the profile summary with you to the interview and score each answer immediately after it is provided, using a simple scale, such as 1-5.
6. Be clear about what classifies an excellent answer at 5 and a poor one at 1.
7. Compare scores of all interviewed candidates as a group to highlight top candidate(s) for the role.

Assessment Tools and Tests

Work sample tests or case studies that mimic the kinds of tasks the candidate will be doing in the job are one of the best indicators of future job performance, as shown in the graph below. Evaluating work sample tests from multiple applicants also helps calibrate your judgment to see how Candidate A compares to Candidate B. A skills test forces you to critique the quality of a candidate's work versus unconsciously judging them based on less reliable criteria, such as personality, interests or appearance.

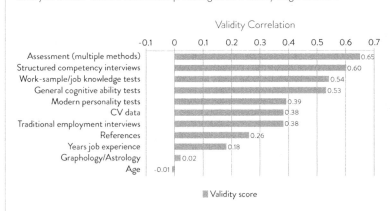

RECRUITMENT BEST PRACTICE:
A MULTI-FACED ASSESSMENT PROCESS

Validity of a multi-faceted assessment process greater than any single measure

Validity Correlation

	Validity score
Assessment (multiple methods)	0.65
Structured competency interviews	0.60
Work-sample/job knowledge tests	0.54
General cognitive ability tests	0.53
Modern personality tests	0.39
CV data	0.38
Traditional employment interviews	0.38
References	0.26
Years job experience	0.18
Graphology/Astrology	0.02
Age	-0.01

Source: British Psychological Society? Accord Group Psychological Bulletin 124; Robertson I. and Smith M. (2010, Personnel Selection; Journal of Occupational and Organisational Psychology

Affinity bias is a constant challenge in the hiring process. We tend to unconsciously award strengths that we ourselves possess when evaluating candidates instead of rewarding the competences and skills that are appropriate for the current role. By complementing your internal assessment process with assessment tools and tests, you will be able to objectively identify and assess the candidate's strengths, areas of development and drive.

Hire by Committee

To ensure you hire the right candidate for the long term, you need to combine individual competency-based interviews with committee-based decision making. As Harvard Professor Iris Bohnet has highlighted in her book *What Works*; "Four interviewers, four data points from four individual interviews trump one data point from one collective interview".[37]

Hiring committees help reduce unconscious bias and provide a more objective review of the data. They can also help to prevent idiosyncrasies of individual interviewers. Your hiring committee should include members of various levels of seniority and representatives from all areas of the business. Also, the members of your hiring committee should receive support and training from HR about interview techniques and the various biases involved in the process. The committee members should receive and review all the information and feedback collected for the relevant candidate. At the committee meeting, all members should share their assessments and comments to facilitate a discussion resulting in a recommendation to HR and/or the hiring manager.

Decision Fatigue

It has been well documented during the past three decades that each successive decision depletes us, leading us to make poorer decisions over time.[38] It is therefore important to structure a streamlined interview process, which doesn't rely too much on any one person to be making decisions about candidates. This is why selecting up front who is going to be involved at each stage and keeping the number of formal interview rounds to the absolute minimum, is so important. When you do this, you will make better decisions than if you overload one or two people with the process responsibility or keep adding additional rounds. This is not to say that additional introductory or coffee meetings across a firm should not happen. Informal meetings and introductions are valuable to give candidates greater insight to a firm's culture and members of the wider team. The important piece to remember is that when these meetings are unstructured and outside of the formal evaluation process, they should not fall into the final assessment of candidates.

Reference Checking

Referrals are often completed too late in the hiring process, by routine, or not at all. However, they are a powerful tool in assessing candidates and increasing the level of inclusivity in your hiring process. For example, it is all too easy for a candidate to claim they are committed to sustainability in an interview. However, if they know that references will check any specific claims they make on important topics, then they are much more likely to tell the truth. It will also provide another objective data point to inform your final decision. Informal or soft references from a diverse set of past team members describing how the candidate helped them on their journey and checking any claims that were made is recommended. The same goes for candidates. One of the most helpful references to take on an employer is speaking with a former employee about the firm and individuals within a team.

Defined Diversity Targets

Affirmative action, such as setting targets, is sometimes disapproved of; critics claim that candidates may be awarded roles because they are from underrepresented groups, rather than because they are competent. However, a study by the London School of Economics (LSE) found the reverse to be true. The LSE study provided a unique window on quotas and pushed forward the measurement of competence in political selection. In 1993, Sweden's Social Democratic party voluntarily introduced a strict gender quota for its candidates. In internal discussions of the reform, the party's Women's branch observed that some men were more critical than others. The quota became known colloquially as the Crisis of the Mediocre Man, since the incompetent men had the most to fear from an influx of women into politics.

Within each local party, they compared the proportion of competent politicians in elections after the quota to the 1991 level. The figure below shows some striking results. The left panel illustrates their estimates for politicians of both genders, with black dots showing the change in the proportion of competent representatives in a party which was forced to increase their share of women (by 100 percentage points). The right panel splits the results by men and women (blue dots for men and pink dots for women). It shows distinctly that the average competence of male politicians increased in the places where the quota had a larger impact, and that the effect is concentrated on the three elections following the quota. On average, a higher female representation by ten percentage points raised the proportion of competent men by three percentage points. For the competence of women, they observed little discernible effect.

ESTIMATED IMPACT OF THE GENDER QUOTA
ON THE FRACTIONS OF COMPETENT POLITICIANS (LEFT)
AND COMPETENT MEN AND WOMEN SEPERATELY (RIGHT)

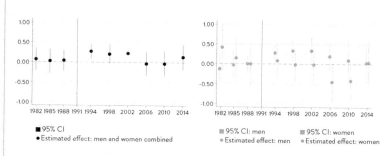

Note: Dots denote point estimates and bars 95% confidence intervals.

Subdividing the men into leaders and followers also revealed another interesting finding. There was clear evidence of a reduction in the proportion of male leaders (those at the top of the ballot) with mediocre competence. This suggests that quotas work in part by shifting incentives in the composing party ballots. Mediocre leaders are either kicked out or resign in the wake of more gender parity; because new leaders – on average – are more competent. They feel less threatened by selecting more able candidates, which starts a virtuous circle of higher competence.

DEBIASED RECRUITMENT
EXERCISE

The Chicago Bulls dominated the 1990s with six NBA championships in eight seasons. A large part of their success has been attributed to the way a highly diverse group of individuals came together as a team on the court. In this image, Chicago Bulls guard Michael Jordan (left) and Scottie Pippen (right) embrace Dennis Rodman (centre) during a game against the Los Angeles Lakers at the United Center at Chicago, Illinois, USA in December 1996. The Bulls defeated the Lakers 129-123 in overtime.

Can you remember an interview where you felt poorly assessed
for the role you were applying for?

How did that make you feel?

What could have been done better?

What areas of your company interview process can be improved based
on the inclusive hiring advice in this chapter?

Communicate the areas for improvement to your leadership,
HR and talent team.

Psychological Safety

The concept of psychological safety is not new. It was first mooted by pioneering scholars in the 1960s and grew in popularity during the 1990s, continuing to do so today. Research by Amy Edmondson and Zhike Lei shows that people who feel psychologically safe tend to be more innovative, learn from their mistakes and are motivated to improve in their work.[39] It is a particularly helpful concept to keep in mind for recruitment. Psychological safety during the interview process is all about creating environments in which candidates feel accepted and respected. There are ways to identify if your process is psychologically safe or unsafe.

For example, in an unsafe environment, it is likely that any mistake you make during an interview will be judged as a failure and limited follow-up questions are asked to help you to achieve a satisfactory answer. In a psychologically safe interview candidates can disclose their own mistakes and failures, and the insights that they have learned from them. Interviewers who are able to create these environments are the ones who demonstrate tolerance of failure by encouraging the candidate to engage in a discussion and learn together. They also encourage candidates to ask for help, clarifications, feedback or information during an interview. These subtle behaviours signal loud and clear to candidates that your organisation cares about inclusion.

THOUGHTS

CHAPTER 6
PURPOSEFUL ACTION
AND POSITIVE RETURNS
ENHANCE BUSINESS VALUES

*"Diversity is being invited to the party;
inclusion is being asked to dance."*
Verna Myers

The spirit of inclusion is about action. The welcome words and
the data gathering agenda are essential first steps. The expert
choreography is in the strategy you create, the roadmap you put in
place and the engagement across the whole business. This chapter
will explore the most robust inclusion and diversity initiatives based
on the latest academic research. Successful delivery of an inclusion
and diversity strategy across your whole business will yield positive
returns. It will allow you to capture the enormous business value of
untapped potential, talent, productivity and innovation internally
and the new consumers, products and markets externally. It will
also ensure that you continue to have a social licence to operate in
a fast-changing and sustainably-minded world. In this world it is
imperative for all businesses to have a purpose, as well as a profit.

Shared Purpose
Looking at inclusion and diversity through a commercial lens is
a huge, but relatively nascent, opportunity for organisations to
differentiate their business and demonstrate their purpose. This
commercial lens is about recognising how you can reach more
talent and more customers, which in turn adds more value and
delivers better returns for your business and its community. When

you conduct this exercise as a business, you are identifying and claiming the 'missing millions' that other companies have ignored.[40] Although every part of your business should be considered through an inclusion and diversity lens, it does not necessarily mean the areas you will prioritise will feature every aspect of your business.

For example, after analysing your business through an inclusion and diversity lens, you may decide the greatest impact is in the talent you are attracting, retaining and promoting versus the customers and clients that you work with, or the partners in your supply chain or your service providers. However, often, you will find that business areas link together. For example, diverse talent is often seeking organisations that have a more representative customer and client base. To have the greatest impact commercially and socially, it is important to focus where you will add the most value.

A Focused Approach
In 2020, Diageo, the global drinks company, decided to add inclusion and diversity as a core strategic focus of their business. Building on the sustainability focused commitments of the previous decade in the areas of responsible drinking and environmental impact, they added targets for inclusion and diversity. The additional focus was a result of applying an inclusion and diversity lens to their entire business. This highlighted their dependence on 'recruiting, retaining and developing diverse talent with a range of backgrounds, skills and capabilities' across the 180 countries where they operate. In addition, they recognised that 'diversity of thought and experience fuels growth and innovation' and brings them 'closer to the consumer base'.

The work that Diageo has completed around gender equality has resulted in the top global ranking by diversity data company Equileap. In 2020, 39 percent of their leadership roles and 55 percent of their board positions were held by women.[41] Their target for 2030 is to achieve gender balance in leadership roles and to have 45 percent ethnically diverse leadership.

Unconscious Bias (UB) Training

One of the strategies that many companies have adopted to address the problem of a lack of diversity is UB training. The time, money, and effort put into UB training by companies globally is estimated to be around $8bn a year.[42] In 2018, Starbucks famously closed 8,000 of its stores to conduct UB training after an incident in which an employee called the police on two potential Black customers. Facebook has demonstrated their commitment to tackling unconscious bias over multiple years and has published their training material online.[43]

Underlying Beliefs

However, the issue with all the focus on UB training is that it is a radical oversimplification of the challenge. Social psychology recognises many types of bias including the things we would do openly if it weren't for the social ramifications, feelings we are aware of but ashamed to admit, information we consciously believe due to genuine ignorance, and beliefs we justify on cultural or other grounds. These concepts have many names – aversive racism, symbolic racism, even colour-blind racism.[44] Sexism is similarly complex covering a number of different concepts like hostile sexism and benevolent sexism.[45] The idea that all, or even most prejudice today is entirely unconscious is simply not true. Unconscious bias is an important piece of the puzzle, but it is not the only one.

Diversity Training

The other difficulty with an exclusive focus on UB training is that it doesn't lead to more diverse teams. In the US, Professors Dobbin and Kalev researched more than 800 companies to see how different diversity programmes affected the proportions of ethnic minorities and women in management. Surprisingly, they found that mandatory diversity training made these companies less diverse, not more diverse, in their management structures. Similarly, Bezrukova and colleagues looked at 260 studies on diversity training, spanning the last 40 years of research on the subject. They found 'no compelling evidence that long-term effects of diversity training are sustainable'.[46] This isn't to say that unconscious bias training serves no purpose at all. It is useful for raising awareness of bias and for giving people the tools to start discussing bias.[47]

But the evidence is very clear; unconscious bias training, by itself, will not make your company any more diverse or inclusive.[48]

POOR RETURNS ON THE USUAL PROGRAMS
THE THREE MOST POPULAR INTERVENTIONS MADE FIRMS LESS DIVERSE, NOT MORE, BECAUSE MANAGERS RESISTED STRONG ARMING

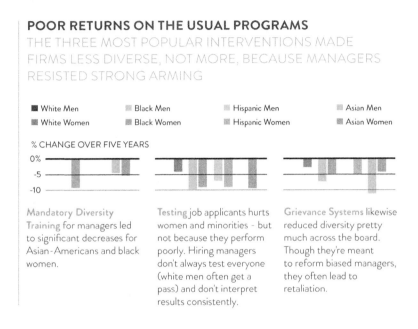

■ White Men   ▨ Black Men   ▨ Hispanic Men   ▨ Asian Men
▨ White Women   ▨ Black Women   ▨ Hispanic Women   ▨ Asian Women

% CHANGE OVER FIVE YEARS

Mandatory Diversity Training for managers led to significant decreases for Asian-Americans and black women.

Testing job applicants hurts women and minorities - but not because they perform poorly. Hiring managers don't always test everyone (white men often get a pass) and don't interpret results consistently.

Grievance Systems likewise reduced diversity pretty much across the board. Though they're meant to reform biased managers, they often lead to retaliation.

Holistic Strategies

Rather than focusing energy on unconscious bias alone, companies need to work holistically on building an inclusive culture and redesigning systems to manage for bias. While the available research doesn't support the long-term effectiveness of UB training alone, it does show that diversity and inclusion can be improved when a number of targeted strategies are applied together.[49] This is especially important for companies operating in major cities, which tend to be more diverse than other parts of the country. For example, 41 percent of Londoners in the UK are Black and minority ethnic, compared to an average of 13 percent in the whole of England.[50]

Affinity Bias

One of the classic biases in recruitment processes is affinity bias, which is often referred to as hiring in your own image. This is a common pitfall, which leads to teams that look the same, sound the same and often have very similar education and work backgrounds. The reason this happens is because as humans we have an innate preference for people who are similar to us. For example, if someone enjoys sports as much as you, it is tempting to spend time together speaking about this during an interview and allowing how much you enjoyed connecting on that subject to cloud your judgement of a candidate. It might also mean you remember more about the aspects of the candidate that were similar to you, rather than the things that were different and could bring more complementary, rather than identical skills and interests into your team.

Greater Bias Awareness

To develop an inclusive culture, it is important for everyone in the organisation to develop an awareness of their own bias. It is through awareness raising coupled with systems redesign that companies can manage the bias that gets in the way of effective decision making and equal access to opportunities. We will explore specific system redesign strategies in more detail in subsequent chapters. At this stage, the critical point is educating yourself on the different types of biases at work and becoming more aware of your own biases, the conscious and the unconscious. This next Reflect and Act exercise has been designed to help you on that journey of greater bias awareness.

BIAS AWARENESS RAISING
EXERCISE

*In June 2020, there were many marches and protests in support of
Black Lives Matter (BLM) around the world. In this moving portrait,
a woman wearing a BLM face mask holds her son whilst saluting
in solidarity at a BLM protest in North Yorkshire, UK.*

REFLECT
Consider your affinity bias at work.

Are there particular people you enjoy working with more than others,
which is irrespective of their objective performance?

What is it that you appreciate and value about them?
How many similarities do you have?

ACT
Complete the Harvard Implicit Association Test (IAT) that measures
attitudes and beliefs that you may or may not be aware of. The IAT is
especially interesting if it shows that you have an implicit attitude that
you did not know about. It is a robust and helpful tool for raising your bias
awareness. To find out more about the methodology and history of the
IAT refer to https://implicit.harvard.edu/implicit/iatdetails.html

Complete your personal IAT test at:
https://implicit.harvard.edu/implicit/

Share the results with someone you trust
and who you can reflect on the results with.

Consider encouraging your wider team to complete the IAT
as part of raising your collective bias awareness.

Commitment to Purpose and Profit

As we have established, an inclusive corporate culture creates an environment where employees thrive, and the bottom line grows. People work best when they feel at ease to be themselves and developing diverse talent reaps rewards, as we have explored in earlier chapters. Increasing engagement gives employees a stake in the company's purpose, promoting professional and personal growth that reduces staff turnover.

These shifts do not happen by chance, they happen with clear intention, action and data. As Freya Williams explained in *Green Giants: How Smart Companies Turn Sustainability Into Billion-Dollar Businesses*, responsible missions and visionary leadership are lucrative.

Companies such as Chipotle, which is the largest restaurant purchaser of sustainable and humanely reared meats, and Natura, which sells sustainable cosmetics, "regard profit as an outcome of achieving their purpose," she wrote. "This philosophy is part of what enables them to outperform their profit and oriented counterparts."[51]

The action of inclusion is not a quick fix and it cannot be achieved in a single afternoon of UB training session. It requires serious and sustained work, at the individual and the corporate level. But it is possible and there are many companies, such as Microsoft, Diageo and Chipotle, who are walking the walk.

THOUGHTS

CHAPTER 7
INCENTIVES
AND ACCOUNTABILITY
CELEBRATE SUCCESS

"Track your small wins to motivate big accomplishments."
Teresa Amabile

When you want your inclusion and diversity strategy to become a reality you need the right incentives in place. Focus on the carrots that will motivate everyone in the organisation to drive inclusive actions. Reserve the sticks for worst case scenarios. All too often there is a blaming and shaming culture around inclusion and diversity, which can hamper progress.

Ongoing engagement from leadership is essential, as is activating the middle management of the company. The more you can engage every level of your business the more likely you are to be successful. Ensuring there is visibility and accountability on the actions you want, will ensure you create the social norms for a more inclusive culture and motivate other people to follow suit. This creates an evergreen environment where employees are empowered to be inclusion and diversity advocates irrespective of their gender, race or creed. Even where there is resistance to the strategy, which there inevitably will be, you have a stronger chance of shifting mindsets with the right incentives in place. Above all, keeping in mind that we are all works-in-progress on this topic, will help maintain motivation and accountability.[52]

Activate Accountability

Accountability can make inclusion efforts more transparent and visible to other people. A large body of literature has shown that social norms influence how we interact with colleagues. We infer what is appropriate and accepted from the behaviour of others.[53] As such, sharing evidence and the positive actions of individuals and teams can help embed inclusion into a company's culture.

In a 2019 study on the effect of social norms on diversity, researchers found that visibility influences how people follow norms, especially when their behaviours are being scrutinised.[54] Participants in this online experiment were assigned the role of a manager hiring a new team member. They were told the HR department within the organisation cared about racial diversity and could review team composition decisions. They were randomly allocated to a team of high visibility within the company or one where there was a low probability that HR would review their decision. As a result, participants were significantly more likely to select a Black candidate when the team was highly visible. It seems that transparency and accountability are effective motivators to move all of us towards positive action.

Make it Visible

Visibility around promotions has been a key tactic that the financial services firm JP Morgan has been using to achieve its inclusion and diversity objectives. At each level of the organisation, there is an expectation that the promotion list should reflect the composition of the population from which promotions are made. This is to ensure that promotions are made with proportionality and representation in mind.

In 2020 the firm published their workforce composition data, including promotions for Vice President and above by gender globally and on ethnicity within the US.[55] Within the US, they were also able to show further areas of diversity across LGBTQ+, Disabilities and Military veterans. Progress on gender is clear to see with an almost equally balanced global workforce and a 22% increase in female board representation in the past 12 months. On ethnicity there had been a single digit increase across all levels, apart from at the board, where there was an 8% decline. This level of transparency allows for accountability and action where required.

Gateways and Pathways

When it comes to driving change on inclusion and diversity, it is helpful to consider the concept of gateways and pathways. In her book *The Person You Mean To Be*, Dolly Chugh describes; "diversity as the gateways to schools, organisations, and communities, and inclusion as the pathways leading up to and after that gateway".

Key people play a disproportionate role in driving diversity in the higher echelons of firms by acting as gatekeepers, directly restricting or enabling entry into positions, as well as setting standards for other people to follow. For instance, an analysis of all CEO female successions in the largest corporations in the US between 1989 and 2009 found that women's success was related to their predecessors promoting gender-inclusive gatekeeping.[56] Ensuring that gatekeepers are carefully chosen and regularly assessed is essential for a company's inclusive agenda.

Turbocharge the Taskforce

Many companies seeking to move strategy into action have created Diversity, Equity and Inclusion (DEI) taskforces or committees with this responsibility.[57] This is a very important stakeholder group. At its best the DEI Taskforce is a voluntary employee group representative of the entire organisation which focuses on informing and implementing the inclusion and diversity strategy. It operates as a think tank and support network for management, as well as holding them accountable to the organisation's commitment and targets. In addition to ensuring all perspectives of the organisation are represented in the DEI work, a taskforce can help promote social accountability. Research by Dobbin and Khalev from Harvard, has shown that on average, companies that put in an DEI Taskforce see a nine percent to 30 percent increase in the representation of White women and ethnic minority groups in management during the following five years.[58]

Key Principles

For an DEI Taskforce to be successful there are a few key principles to follow, as listed below.

1. Taskforce membership should be based on a voluntary and rotating basis.
2. Ensure all parts of the organisation, levels of seniority and minorities are represented.
3. Taskforce leaders should sit on the executive team and have deep experience overseeing teams and high-profile projects.
4. Work closely with the company inclusion and diversity strategy, set goals, roles and responsibilities.
5. If there is no strategy in place when the task force is formed, then this is the first task to focus on and achieve full management engagement.
6. Regularly report into the board with full executive support and budget allocation to deliver on your goals.
7. Learn your company's historical context and stay on top of its DEI data.
8. Track and review progress. Share this as widely as possible with the business, not only with the management and the board.
9. Celebrate success!

Melt the Middle

Middle managers can play a crucial role in translating corporate priorities into practice for employees on the front lines. The engagement of managers is critical because they set the tone for the engagement of the people who report to them. According to research from Gallup in 2020, managers affected 70 percent of the variance in team engagement.[59] They are responsible for keeping employees informed about what is going on in the organisation, setting priorities, and providing ongoing feedback and accountability. The same research showed that employee engagement is an even stronger predictor of performance during tough periods, such as economic recessions and global pandemics.

"Without the engagement and education of your middle management your inclusion efforts are unlikely to remain on track."

If managers are only paying lip service to diversity, then they can undermine efforts to attract, retain and develop an inclusive and diverse workforce. Many of these managers may be well-meaning. Their lack of commitment to inclusion and diversity may stem from habits dating back decades, or to their own struggles to do more with less. Research from Equality Group in 2019 found that 47 percent of London professionals wanted managers to receive more training and support to create an inclusive environment at work.[60] In the same research, 30 percent of London-based managers acknowledged their need for upskilling on the topic. This sobering reality highlights the importance of helping middle managers embrace the idea of diversity and inclusion as a strategic imperative and upskilling and equipping them in the process. Without the engagement and education of your middle management your inclusion efforts are unlikely to remain on track.

The work of Equality Group has shown that the way to melt middle management resistance is with relevant data and contextualised stories from their own organisation. One of the ways to gather the data and stories required is through a combination of a tailored 360 digital survey with specific inclusion and diversity questions. Alongside the survey, one-to-one interviews help to extract compelling and insightful stories and provide examples of the current state of play in the organisation. The assessment process, the resulting information and the education developed sparks greater self-awareness, commitment and accountability for managers. The results are significant. In 2020, 95 percent of participants in the Inclusion Programme at Equality Group believed their organisation will be more inclusive as a result. This is a significant improvement on data from Glassdoor in 2019 showing that 50 percent of employees do not believe their organisations are doing enough about inclusion and diversity.[61]

Offer Real Incentives
To ensure you are able to deliver on your inclusion and diversity ambitions, you need to be clear on the expectations entailed. DEI efforts should be measured with the same scrutiny as any other business objectives. This is why measuring the data, as outlined in Chapter 4 and developing a clear strategy, as outlined in Chapter 5, are critical stages to complete. By identifying and setting time-bound actions you will avoid excuses that DEI is not measurable. The expectations and goals need to be clearly communicated and easily accessible to everyone. This is because visibility is motivating and spurs the level of accountability you want across the organisation.

Progress on your DEI targets and ambitions should be linked to the remuneration of the management team and relevant team members. If you don't hold key decision-makers accountable, you are in practice signalling that DEI is not a business priority, and certainly not significant enough to link to any financial reward. If you are serious about inclusion, equity and diversity in your business, it must have a financial benefit attached to it.

"If you are serious about inclusion and diversity in your business, it must have a financial benefit attached to it."

Annual Targets
According to research by Deloitte in 2017, only 6 percent of companies tie annual compensation to diversity outcomes.[62] This is despite 78 percent of companies believing diversity and inclusion is a competitive advantage. However, there are firms leading by example, by linking compensation to diversity targets. For instance,

the Swedish investment management firm, Kinnevik decided in 2018 to link DEI targets into annual corporate targets. In turn, these targets were integrated into all team members' individual objectives. The achievement of individual objectives and the overall corporate targets influence all employees' remuneration. They also measure annually the quality of managers' leadership style in relation to DEI through the performance process, which forms part of the basis of their individual compensation.

Balanced Scorecard

Another positive example is Sodexo, the French food services and facilities management company, who use a Diversity Index and Balanced Scorecard linked to bonus compensation to improve accountability for its DEI ambitions. The scorecard, which accounts for 15 percent of the executive team's bonus and between 10 and 15 percent of managers' bonuses, rates leaders' diversity efforts on a series of metrics. 60 percent of the diversity scorecard is focused on hard numbers, how many women and minorities were hired, promoted and retained. The other 40 percent is focused on promoting inclusive behaviours. This link between compensation and DEI goals has been the driving force behind improving DEI at Sodexo.

INCLUSIVE INCENTIVES
EXERCISE

Queen's set at Live Aid in 1985 has often been hailed as one of the greatest performances seen at Wembley Stadium, in London UK. Freddie Mercury's spectacular vocals and theatrics on the stage were some of the defining moments of his musical career. They were a true celebration of life and creativity.

REFLECT

In what ways are you incentivised to be more inclusive at work?

Reflect on your intrinsic motivation for inclusion and diversity,
as well as external motivating factors.

Which ones have been most motivating for you?

ACT

If you are one of the 50 percent who believe your organisation
could be doing more when it comes to inclusion and diversity,
let your leaders know. If you are a leader or a manager,
engage your peers in the education process.

If your organisation is yet to fully upskill on the topic of inclusion and
diversity consider the Equality Group Inclusion Education series.

Celebrate Small Wins

A powerful and simple way to motivate everyone across your organisation about inclusion and diversity progress is to celebrate the small wins. Research by Harvard Professor and Author Teresa Amabile has shown that tracking these small and incremental wins can do wonders for motivation and boost self-confidence.[63] In fact, as much as the big wins do. This is because every achievement—big or small—activates the brain's reward circuitry. The pathway opens up and we receive the deeply satisfying release of testosterone and dopamine which leaves us feeling energised, confident and motivated.

Small wins can be as important or even more important than the big ones. There are two main reasons for this. Firstly, without the small wins, the big ones are less likely to happen. We get demoralised and can suffer from diversity fatigue. The small wins hold the key to momentum. They infuse us with motivation to keep going. Secondly, the big magical moments that we have written into the overall vision happen so infrequently. Those big, breakthrough moments, such as achieving gender balance on the management team may take longer to realise. Small wins are more frequent. What they lack in size they make up for in numbers. Acknowledging the small wins, a little more at work is essential. In fact, we have to do more than acknowledge them, we need to celebrate them. They hold the key to long-term inclusion and diversity success.

THOUGHTS

CHAPTER 8
REVIEWS, RETENTION AND PROMOTION
REACH FOR PARITY

"I always say that talent and capability is everywhere, all it needs is opportunity."
Kathrine Switzer

Once you have built a diverse team, the last thing you want is to lose them. Unfortunately, this happens at many companies. The 'leaky pipeline' is a challenge across all industries. Multiple research studies have shown starkly higher attrition rates among underrepresented groups, especially as you progress up the hierarchy. It is also the primary cause of the many pay gaps that persist. If we cannot secure our most talented, diverse talent into senior executive positions, with the highest compensation packages, then we will never close the gaps. Part of the solution is to ensure frequent, objective and transparent review practices. In addition, equal access to information and resources, with a recognition of the full range of employee contributions supports higher retention. The combination means glass ceilings can be broken and leaky pipelines can be fixed.

Shatter the Ceiling

'The glass ceiling' is a term most frequently applied to women unable to achieve promotions and fair pay because of a biased occupational system. In reality, a ceiling exists whenever someone is unfairly kept from advancement and fair pay because of sex, race, age, religion, or sexual orientation. The glass ceiling is a reality faced by millions of professionals every day: qualified people who, for arbitrary reasons, do not gain the pay and promotions they deserve.

Pay inequities occur on many different fronts: from unequal pay for equal work; to opportunity gaps preventing people from attaining leadership roles; and unequal wage growth widening pay gaps at higher age groups and job levels. Throughout all of these metrics, White, well-educated, able-bodied, heterosexual men maintain an edge over other groups. According to a study conducted by the Kapor Center for Social Impact in 2017, women of colour face the starkest pay disparities, with professional women of colour earning nearly half of the salary of White and Asian males.[64] Factors including: a lack of transparency; individual biases; and lack of preventative laws and policies, contribute to the persistent pay gap.

Acknowledge the Ambition
One pernicious myth that continues to exist in the business world is that there is a lack of diversity at the top due to a lack of ambition to be there. However, when you look at the underlying evidence, there is no shortage of career ambition among underrepresented groups. Women, ethnic minorities, LGBTQ+ employees all share a deep drive to reach the top of organisations.

According to a study by Equality Group, 59 percent of ethnic minority professionals in the UK aspire to senior management and board level positions in their future.[65] This is significantly higher than the 14 percent of White professionals with a similar ambition. In the US, a study by SurveyMonkey in 2020 showed that 89 percent of women are ambitious to succeed in their careers, with only ten percent stating they were "not so ambitious" or "not ambitious at all".[66]

"If companies can do their inner work, then they will save individual minorities having to do it for them."

This challenges the thesis of Facebook COO Sheryl Sandberg who wrote the book: *Lean In: Women, Work, and the Will to Lead.* A key concept in the book is the Women's Leadership Ambition Gap, which are the inner obstacles women must overcome to reach higher levels of executive management. From Sandberg's perspective, this is what accounts for the poor representation of women in top leadership positions. She explains that; "when jobs are described as powerful, challenging and involving high levels of responsibility, they appeal to more men than women".[67] However, as we have seen in Chapter 3, inclusive language is critical to attracting diverse talent. In 2021, why do we need to describe senior leadership roles as powerful and challenging? Why couldn't we describe them as collaborative and enabling?

With the growing need for inclusive leadership across industries, what we need to be seeking in our leaders is greater empathy, courage, humility and collaboration. If they were the qualities that are valued, rewarded and achieve promotions in companies, then maybe women wouldn't need to do as much of the inner work as previously thought. If companies can do their inner work, then they will save individual minorities having to do it for them.

Fix the System

Despite the focus on the inner work of success, the outer work of the system is arguably more important. Great progress has been made in documenting how review and promotion best practice can improve workplace equality. In performance reviews, an increase in transparency and visibility has shown several benefits. A longitudinal study looked at performance-based reward decisions before and after a firm introduced accountability and transparency procedures.[68] Before the procedures were introduced there was a significantly different gap in merit-based pay by gender, race and foreign nationality compared with White men receiving the same performance evaluation. After the policy, once managers realised that their decisions would be compared to other divisions, there was a reduction in this pay gap. Transparency in reporting can make disparities easier to spot and to correct. The use of data and auditing can also encourage managers themselves, to review how they allocate resources within the team and encourage self-correction.

Consider the Biases

As with the hiring process, there are a number of biases that operate throughout traditional review and promotion practices. Iris Bohnet at Harvard has shown that there is a strong bias towards overestimating men's future potential and underestimating women's future potential. Women and minorities are often assessed on historic performance and are underestimated for future potential. This is especially true in male-dominated industries, such as financial services.

Emilio Castilla at MIT has studied performance reward bias for many years. His research shows that even when employees achieve the same evaluation score, White men will be paid more than women or other minority groups. When giving feedback, individuals tend to focus more on the personality and attitudes of women. Contrarily, they focus more on the behaviours and accomplishments of men. Janice Fanning Maden at Wharton has built on this point to show that men are often staffed on higher-value accounts and projects than women, which contributes to a widening gender pay gap.[69] This exacerbates gender bias, promotion opportunities, as well as the pay gap.

One of the most unfortunate biases that comes into effect during reviews is the Idiosyncratic Rater Effect. A 1998 study in Personnel Psychology found that more than 60 percent of a manager's rating was actually a reflection of the individual manager, not the employee being rated.[70] In addition, they found that more than half of the variance associated with ratings had more to do with the quirks of the person giving the rating than the person being rated. Rater bias was the biggest predictor. It held more weight than actual performance, the performance dimension being rated, the rater's perspective, and even measurement error. This suggests that a review tells us more about the reviewer than the person being reviewed. A further study in the Journal of Applied Psychology in 2000 demonstrated that managers rate people higher in skills where they are not as proficient themselves.[71] Conversely, they rate other people lower in activities they have excelled at. In other words, managers weigh their performance evaluations toward personal eccentricities, rather than objective measures.

"Idiosyncratic rater effect: a review tells us more about the reviewer than the person being reviewed."

Equalise Access

Alongside the many biases that exist in the standard review and promotion practice, there is also a lack of equal access to essential information and resources. These processes are often run either without a set of formal rules to guide them or with only a certain set of people understanding them.[72] Additional research has found that gender and ethnic differences between supervisors and subordinates can often result in the subordinate being under-resourced.[73] This can lead to employee dissatisfaction, burnout and high turnover. This need has only increased with the majority of people moving to remote working, where there is no guarantee that everyone has the same level of equipment, use of technology tools, or document access as each other. Fortunately, there are simple solutions to this issue. Using a standardised, transparent review system that is clearly documented and circulated to everyone takes away the guesswork and fluctuating estimations of managers. It also ensures that employees all receive the same access across positions.

See the Invisible

Information and resources are not the only things that are passed around informally. Every organisation has a certain amount of invisible work, including: scheduling team calls; organising group catch-ups; sharing inspirational content or interesting reading material; and completing all the informal activities that go unrecognised in reviews. These tasks have great value to an organisation's culture and smooth operation, but rarely is someone promoted for accomplishing them.

Unfortunately, research shows that these invisible tasks are usually not distributed evenly throughout an organisation. Women tend to be given and to volunteer for many more of these invisible tasks than men do.[74] Recent research also reveals similar patterns for ethnic minority workers compared to White workers.[75] The over-allocation of invisible work takes away from an employee's time to perform the important, visible duties that lead to promotion and increase satisfaction at work. It is therefore well worth an employer's time to make this work as visible as possible. Explicitly acknowledging invisible work and distributing it evenly throughout an organisation makes your workplace a fairer and happier place to be.

Reinvent Reviews
Based on the deeply biased nature of most review processes many companies have chosen a more radical route. Adobe, for instance, has abandoned the traditional performance reviews used to assess its 11,000 employees. It calculated that the annual process required 80,000 hours of time from its 2,000 managers, the equivalent of 40 full-time staff.[76] The monumental effort invariably produced poor results, with internal surveys showing that staff felt less inspired and motivated after the appraisal episodes.

The company has instead embraced frequent check-ins, during which managers provide coaching and advice. Check-ins are designed to communicate simply what is expected of staff and to allow managers to give and receive feedback, assist employees with performance improvement, and guide them in their growth and development. This process provides feedback that is more immediate and relevant than the once-a-year, and usually much-dreaded, review. All managers receive extensive training in how to conduct coaching conversations, provide and receive feedback via classes and by role playing realistic, and sometimes difficult, situations.

Achieve Parity

Following the radical reinvention of reviews, and other proactive inclusion and diversity initiatives, Adobe has achieved impressive results. It is a company that has demonstrated gender pay parity since 2018 and ethnicity pay parity since 2020. It is also one of the few companies that is reporting data on what it calls Opportunity Parity. This is the practice of examining fairness in promotions and horizontal movement among demographic groups. The company describes this as a 'long journey' where they had to work hard to 'accurately measure the right dynamics'. In their first year of reporting, they were able to show almost equal opportunity parity between gender and ethnicity, as per the chart below.

OPPORTUNITY PARITY METRICS - FY2020 THROUGH Q3
(DECEMBER 2019 - AUGUST 2020)

	Female	Male	U.S. URM	U.S. non-URM
Promotions	16.8%	16.5%	15.0%	14.9%
Horizontal movement	5.8%	4.6%	6.7%	5.2%
Internal movement*	21.9%	20.5%	20.6%	19.4%

* Internal movement includes promotions and horizontal movement. Employees who experienced both types of movement during FY20 year-to-date were only counted once

Critically, Adobe has taken the step of debiasing their process, measuring their data, publishing it and being held accountable. It is an impressive step ahead of many companies today.

REDESIGN REVIEWS
EXERCISE

The statue of Women's Rights campaigner Dame Millicent Garrett Fawcett GBE is seen in Parliament Square in London, England. She campaigned for women's suffrage through legal change and from 1897 to 1919 led Britain's largest women's rights association, the National Union of Women's Suffrage Societies (NUWSS).

REFLECT

What was the best review you ever received?

What made it so good?

How did the inner work and the outer work come together?

ACT

Improve the system; how evolved is your company review
and promotion practice?

Have you engaged with HR on this topic?
Why not send them an excerpt of this chapter for discussion?

What about hosting a lunch and learn session for your company
on this topic?

Amplification

Researchers have found that in business meetings, where decisions need to be made quickly, it is men who speak more than women.[77] On top of this, despite the common misconception that women are more talkative than men, the critical influence on talkativeness is not gender, but the context and the audience.[78] This means that women are more likely to talk more to other women, but less if they are the minority in the room. Men are also more likely to be more talkative in a room full of men. The bottom line is that if you are a minority in the room, it is less likely that your voice will be heard. You therefore need the help of other people to amplify your voice. Amplification is the practice of noticing when a minority in a group discussion makes a good point, repeating it to give greater emphasis to the point and finally crediting the person who originally made it. If this is done systematically in meetings, it can help counter inherent group and social biases that manifest themselves through who receives the most airtime, recognition and praise. For example, President Obama's White House team credited the evolution from two-thirds men as top aides in 2009, to gender parity by 2014, in large part to the practice of amplification.

How Can You Amplify?
- In a meeting, ask directly a person from a representative minority group their opinion.
- Encourage someone from a minority group to share their opinion as early in the discussion as possible, especially on virtual meetings
- Never interrupt a person from a representative minority group when they are speaking.
- Acknowledge the point that person has made and ask follow up questions.
- When meeting in person, invite a representative from a minority group to sit closer to the front instead of at the sidelines.

THOUGHTS

CHAPTER 9
POSITIVE POLICIES
INCLUSIVE FOUNDATIONS

|

"The loftier the building, the deeper must the foundations be laid."
Thomas à Kempis

|

Positive policies are the firm foundations of an inclusive business. Policies serve a vital purpose in supporting and protecting an organisation and its people. They create boundaries for acceptable behaviour within the workplace and serve as a guideline for best practice in particular work situations. They are part of the essential infrastructure that articulates the overall inclusion and diversity values of the company. At the same time, more progressive policies can enable your business to stand out from the crowd as an inclusive leader. If you want your business to be a place where diverse talent can thrive for the long term, then you need to go beyond the statutory minimum. Thoughtful and generous policies, contextualised for locations and cultures, will go a long way in reflecting what you value and the behaviour you want to encourage.

Declare Equality
The first foundation stone to lay is your equal employment opportunity (EEO) statement. This is one of the core ways you communicate that you value inclusion and diversity at your company. The wording can be used across all your employment materials, including: job descriptions; employee handbooks; your digital channels, and anywhere you want to communicate your inclusive values. A good example of an EEO statement is Survey Monkey, which has one of the most diverse boards in technology, including entrepreneur and

elite tennis player Serena Williams and Sheryl Sandberg, the COO of Facebook. They take a short and simple non-legalistic approach and mention two key words: 'diversity' and 'inclusive': *"SurveyMonkey is an equal opportunity employer. We celebrate diversity and are committed to creating an inclusive environment for all employees."*[79] However, it is important to keep in mind that recent research has shown that EEO statements in isolation can backfire.[80] Without clear commitment and action, these words can very quickly become empty, tokenistic and disingenuous.

Demonstrate Care

The next part of the foundations are your anti-discrimination and anti-harassment policies. These are critical for ensuring fair and equitable behaviour, which is still lacking at many corporates. According to a study conducted by the Kapor Center for Social Impact in 2017, 53 percent of women in technology experience harassment at work, compared to 16 percent of men. At the same time, men of colour are 40 percent more likely to leave a firm due to unfair treatment. Negative experiences and unfair treatment are significantly related to turnover in companies and employee burnout. They contribute to the lack of diversity by creating a revolving door for underrepresented groups. Effective anti-discrimination policies show that a company cares about the priorities and wellbeing of everyone at their firm. A study by Boston Consulting Group in 2018 of more than 16,500 employees worldwide, demonstrated that effectively worded and transparent anti-discriminatory policies are one of the most necessary and effective ways of establishing inclusion and diversity in the workplace.[81] In fact, it was ranked as the number one most effective diversity initiative by everyone in the organisation, irrespective of gender, ethnicity or sexuality, as shown in the table below.[82]

THE MOST EFFECTIVE DIVERSITY INITIATIVES

Ranked by everyone

Getting back to basics: fundamentally reducing bias

- Antidiscrimination policies
- Formal training to mitigate biases and increase cultural competency
- Removing bias from evaluation and promoting decisions

For female employees	For employees of color	For LGBTQ employees
Showing a vialable path forward ○ visible role models **Providing tools that help successfully balance career and family responsibilities** ○ flexible-work programs ○ parental leave ○ appropriate health care ○ childcare	**Recruiting a diverse workforce** ○ blind screening ○ diverse interviews panels **Advancing employees of color** ○ bias-free day-to-day experience ○ formal sponsorship of individuals; individual action plans	**Mainstreaming the LGBTQ experience** ○ participating in external events ○ appropriate health care **Removing bias** ○ bias-free day-to-day experience ○ structural interventions

- Back-to-basics measures   - Proven measures   - Hidden gems

Source: BCG Global Diversity Study 2018.

Global Context

Despite positive progress on anti-discrimination in many parts of the world, we are nowhere near an equitable or global approach. The LGBTQ+ community is especially vulnerable to discrimination and violence in many countries. Same-sex acts are illegal in 71 countries and 2.8 billion people live in countries where consensual same-sex acts are a crime.[83]

Even between more progressive nations, such as the UK and the US, there is a wide disparity. Of the top UK firms listed in the FTSE 100, 80 percent make no mention of transgender staff in their non-discrimination policies. In addition, 47 percent of these firms fail to reference protection policies for gay, lesbian or bisexual employees.[84] Today in the US, 75 percent of companies have non-discrimination policies that explicitly reference gender identity, and 93 percent have policies that cover sexual orientation.[85]

Economic Outperformance
There is a significant body of research linking policies aimed at achieving equality to positive economic outcomes. Open for Business has produced several reports showing that open, inclusive and diverse societies experience more economic growth and that discrimination on the basis of sexual orientation or gender identity can damage long-term economic prospects. A global analysis of cities conducted in 2019, showed that higher LGBTQ+ inclusion is correlated with higher city GDP per capita. The regression line suggests a stronger uplift in the move from very low to medium inclusion scores (from dangerous or hostile, to tolerance not inclusion). An outlier in the graph below is Singapore, a city with high GDP per capita but a medium inclusion score. It is still a country which has no specific laws banning workplace harassment.

CITY LGBT+ INCLUSION AND GDP PER CAPITA®

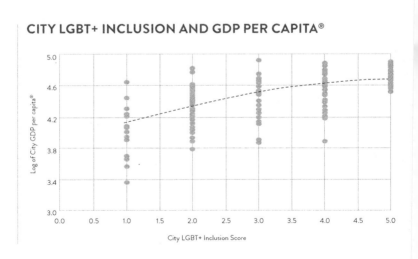

Similar findings came out of a World Bank report in 2020. The research showed that reforming discriminatory laws against women is associated with a smaller gender pay gap, higher levels of female entrepreneurship and better access to finance for women (figure 1.2).[86] Furthermore, raising the retirement age of women to match that of men is correlated with an increased female labour supply, which facilitates larger pensions and better financial security for women of retirement age and their families. Their analysis shows that where the law ensures greater equality of economic opportunity between women and men, female labour force participation is higher. Notably, this result remains after taking into account important factors including income levels, fertility rates, and female education. The countries that scored the highest were Belgium, Canada, Denmark, France, Iceland, Latvia, Luxembourg and Sweden.

WHERE THE WOMEN, BUSINESS AND THE LAW INDEX SHOWS GREATER EQUALITY, FEMALE LABOR FORCE PARTICIPATION RATES ARE HIGHER AND THE WAGE GAP BETWEEN WOMEN AND MEN IS LOWER

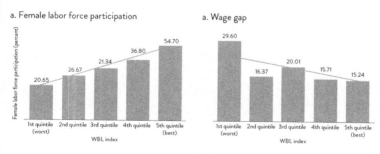

Sources: Panel a: *Women, Business and the Law* (WBL) database; World Development Indicators (WDI) database. Panel b: *Women, Business and the Law* (WBL) database; World Development Indicators (WDI) database; ILOSTAT; OECD.Stat. Note: Panel a: The relationship between the WBL index and female labor force participation is statistically significant after controlling for income (measured as GDP per capita provided in the WDI database), fertility rates, industrial composition, female education, the male working-age population, and the economy-level and time fixed effects. Regression of female labor force participation on the WBL index includes 176 economies for the period 1991-201, as determined by data availability. This statistical relationship should not be interpreted as causal. For full results of the emperical analysis of the relationship between WBL scores and women's economic outcomes, see Hyland, Djankov, and Goldberg (2019). Panel b: The relationship between the WBL index and the gender wage gap is statistically significant after controlling for income (measured as GDP per capita provided in the WDI database), fertility rates, industrial composition, female education, the male working-age population, and economy-level and time fixed effects. Regression of the gender wage gap on the WBL index includes 68 economies for the period 1973-2017, as determined by data availability. The gender wage gap represents the ratio of male to female earnings. This statistical relationship should not be interpreted as causal.

Ensure Equality Training

For positive policies to be most effective in the workplace, they need to be reinforced with regular and relevant training. This is not only to transform what is written down on paper into everyday behaviour, but also to ensure that an employer has a reasonable defence if and when there is a claim against them. In the UK, a common and costly mistake that businesses make is believing that anti-discrimination and anti-harassment policies are enough to trigger the statutory defence enshrined in law. In fact, having an up-to-date policy is only the starting point. Employment tribunals expect employers to pay more than lip service to policies: anti-discriminatory policies need to be backed up with more concerted action, such as regular training. Equality training should be part of the annual learning and development calendar for all staff, from the most senior to the most junior. Ideally, it is also included as part of the onboarding process for new joiners to demonstrate from the outset the organisation's commitment to an inclusive working environment with zero tolerance to discrimination.

"For positive policies to be most effective in the workplace, they need to be reinforced with regular and relevant training."

Move From Threats To Insights

When companies experience cases of discrimination and harassment, there is typically a highly legalistic grievance mechanism in place to manage the process. Although these are intended to protect employees, they can often have adverse consequences. In the US, approximately half of all discrimination and harassment complaints lead to some type of retaliation from managers.[87] Research has also shown that employees who complain about harassment are more likely to end up facing career challenges or experiencing worse mental and physical health compared to similar workers who were harassed, but did not complain.[88] This suggests there is something that is not working about the current grievance systems.

Sociologists Frank Dobbin from Harvard University and Alexandra Kalev from Tel Aviv University have an innovative alternative to legalistic grievance mechanisms. They suggest establishing third party support for employees called Employee Assistance Plans (EAPs), which are run by external parties and offer free and confidential advice to employees. Currently EAPs are not used very often to handle discrimination and harassment issues. If their scope were expanded to provide valuable support and guidance to employees on strategies and tactics around harassment and discrimination, they could serve as an important resource for employees and employers. The key to this type of shift is changing leadership mindsets from seeing complaints as threats to valuing them as insights that can spark positive organisational change.

"The key to this type of shift is changing leadership mindsets from seeing complaints as threats to valuing them as insights that can spark positive organisational change."

Progress Parental Leave
Parental leave is a fundamental policy that encourages greater equality at work. Maternity and Paternity Leave policies need equal consideration. Unfortunately, there is still a long way to go in the corporate sector. A study by Mercer in 2016 found that more than half (52 percent) of companies had no global Parental Leave Policy.[89] Of the companies surveyed only seven percent had a global policy

that covered all four types of leave, including: maternity; paternity; adoption; and parental. Surprisingly, the US is one of the only advanced economies without a law that guarantees paid family leave. In fact, a study by sociologist Michelle J. Budig found that for every child a working American woman has, her salary goes down by four percent, while men generally benefit from having children because employers tend to value fatherhood.[90]

One of the biggest stumbling blocks around parental leave is not only the lack of equal policies, but also the lack of equal uptake among men and women. There are multiple benefits to fathers taking their full parental leave. Fathers develop a strengthened bond with their children. Mothers are able to combine work and family life, by having fathers' involvement in childcare and housework.[91] Finally, and significantly, it promotes the long-term well-being of their children.[92] A study by Eirini Flouri and Ann Buchanan from Oxford University showed that fathers' involvement with their children at age seven protected them against psychological issues later in adolescence. Furthermore, fathers' involvement at age 16 protected against adult psychological distress in women in later life.

Despite all the known benefits of fathers taking parental leave, there is still very low participation even in the most developed economies. In the UK, Shared Parental Leave (SPL) policies were introduced in 2015. The benefit allows couples to share up to 50 weeks of leave and 37 weeks of statutory shared parental pay between them. However, by 2020 data, only two percent of eligible couples had chosen to make use of the scheme.[93] There are a few reasons behind this exceptionally low figure. Firstly, many employers still fail to enhance paternity pay alongside maternity leave, which means there is a serious financial trade-off involved. Secondly, there is still widespread concern about career penalties for men who take their paternity leave. Finally, there is a lack of awareness around what is available for fathers, and also varying levels of social stigma that exist in many countries.[94]

"The myth that you have to be in the office to be a respected and productive team member has now been busted."

Hybrid Working

Working from home or teleworking during the pandemic has ushered in a new era for flexible working policies. What was once deemed impossible for many firms, has been made possible with Covid-19. PwC's Remote Work Survey asked US financial services companies about the topic in June 2020. It found 69 percent of employers expect almost two-thirds of their workforce to be working from home once a week after Covid-19, compared to 29 percent before the pandemic.[95] Google, Salesforce, Facebook and PayPal are among the companies extending full-time remote working through to 2022, while Japanese tech firm Fujitsu is halving its office space and giving its 80,000 employees in the country unprecedented flexibility. Moving forward, the traditional office set-up will give way to a more hybrid work environment. In this arrangement, there will be a rotation between people working from home and those coming into the office. As a result, remote workers will no longer be second class members of the workforce. This is especially good news for employees with disabilities and caring responsibilities.

Physical office space will no doubt remain an important part of the overall work environment, especially for relationship building and collaboration with team members. However, the myth that you have to be in the office to be a respected and productive team member has now been busted.

PROGRESSIVE POLICIES
EXERCISE

In this image, we see from left, Paul Hendricks, brand responsibility analyst, Tasha Woodworth, associate designer, and Pasha Whitmire, material developer, head towards the waves at the surf spot known as C Street during a lunchtime surf break from work at the Patagonia corporate headquarters in Ventura, California on Friday, September 19, 2014.

REFLECT

Which positive policies have you benefited from most in your career?

How consistent have they been across your employment?

Which ones have helped to drive inclusion and diversity?

ACT

From the positive policies in this chapter, are there any missing
in your workplace?

Could you raise this issue with the leadership and HR team?

What is the most progressive policy you have heard of in recent years?

Can you suggest it to your business and to Equality Group
at hello@equality.group. The more we share best practice with each
other, the more we can collectively drive change.

Fundamental Flexibility

Flexibility is an effective approach to take to many policies at work, not only for work location. Patagonia has an aptly named Flexitime Policy called: Let My People Go Surfing. This allows employees to work flexible hours as long as the work is achieved with no negative impact on co-workers. Workers take advantage of this policy to "catch a good swell, go bouldering for an afternoon, pursue an education, or arrive home in time to greet the kids when they climb down from the school bus." They also have a 100 percent retention rate for new mothers, which they credit to their in-house childcare centres, which have been in place since the 1980s.

In another example of flexibility, Spotify implemented a Flexible Public Holidays Policy, to create holiday equity among employees. With more than 90 different nationalities spread across the world, not everyone's heritage and beliefs match the public holiday schedule of the country they currently work in. The policy allows all employees to make a day-off trade: work on a day that is a public holiday in the country where they are employed and take another workday as a holiday instead. For example, someone working in Italy, where Christmas Day is a public holiday, can work that day and trade it for a different day off, for example, Yom Kippur or Diwali.

●

THOUGHTS

CHAPTER 10
HUMANISE WORK
SOCIAL SUSTAINABILITY

"I've learned that people will forget what you said, people will forget what you did, but people will never forget how you made them feel."
Maya Angelou

There is a deeply human element to our work. Without people, there would be no need for organisations. Embedding inclusion, diversity and equity into teams will increase the personal and relational dimension of business. It will also bring with it all the complexity of our humanity. A wide variety of perspectives, biases and priorities, along with debate, disagreement and potentially dissent. Building organisational strength and resilience to manage the increased emotional and psychological range is essential. Although this is not an easy task, there are many techniques and tools that can be learnt and harnessed for long-term diversity success. At a time when the boundaries between work and home have been completely removed by a global pandemic, the benefits of an inclusive culture and an environment that welcomes diversity have the potential to bear even more fruit. Ultimately, paying attention to the emotional and personal aspects of work is going to lead to greater professional fulfilment for everyone.

Expect Innovation
Innovation is one of the many positive results of increasing diversity. Several research studies have shown the innovation benefits of diverse teams. Business professors Cristian Deszö of the University of Maryland and David Ross of Columbia University studied the

effect of gender diversity on the top firms in Standard & Poor's Composite 1500 list, a group designed to reflect the overall US equity market. They measured the firms' 'innovation intensity" through the ratio of research and development expenses to assets. They found that companies which prioritised innovation saw greater financial gains when women were part of the top leadership ranks.[96] A similar case study has been shared by Wanda Hope, the Chief Diversity Officer at Johnson & Johnson (J&J), who has described the innovation that has come out of their multi-cultural and multi-faith teams. For example, Listerine, a J&J product, typically contains alcohol like most mouthwash products. In predominately Muslim cultures, this creates significant issues. A forward-thinking and diverse team out of Malaysia decided to create one that was green tea based and alcohol-free. When it was launched, it increased the market share of Listerine by seven percent. It is a tangible example of diverse teams innovating with new perspectives and market leading products.

"Paying attention to the emotional and personal aspects of work is going to lead to greater professional fulfilment for everyone."

Deal with Difficulties

It is important to acknowledge that diversity in the workplace can create friction. It forces people to work harder, challenges their assumptions and makes them less sure of themselves. Research from the software group Cloverpop found that when decisions are made by homogeneous groups and executed by diverse teams, friction increases by 15 percent.[97] Sadly, this is the case at many organisations, where there is a 'pyramid' structure with less diversity at the senior levels and more at the junior. However, there is a simple way to solve this problem, make the pyramid a cylinder by changing who is part of the decision-making process. The same research showed that when diverse teams were part of both the deciding and the doing, they delivered results 60 percent above the average.

Increasing diversity in decision-making meetings and committees is a quick-win solution to increasing representation and innovation. In 2006, Stanford researcher Katherine Phillips and Margaret Neale of the University of Illinois examined the impact of racial diversity on small decision-making groups in an experiment where sharing information was a requirement for success.[98] The groups with racial diversity significantly outperformed the groups with no racial diversity. Being with similar people leads us to think we all hold the same information and share the same perspective. This is what stopped the all-White groups from effectively processing the information and hindered their creativity and innovation.

The important point to remember is that when we hear dissent from someone who is different from us, it provokes more thought than when it comes from someone who looks like us. However, it is not always an easy social process and requires effective communication and emotional intelligence to navigate well. At the same time, this hard work of dealing with people who are different to us and having interactions that are a little less comfortable can become the irritant that creates the pearl. It can be what sparks that amazing new idea or corrects a mistaken assumption. But it is not always the case that people leave discussions in diverse groups saying it felt great. Allowing space for the additional discussions and reflection is extremely important if you want to see the benefits of diversity. Although the process may take a little longer, it is much more likely to be higher quality than the groupthink process.

"The hard work of dealing with people who are different to us and having interactions that are a little less comfortable can become the irritant that creates the pearl."

Inclusive Meetings

Meetings are a unique insight into the culture of any organisation. MIT Sloan Management research suggests that meetings have increased in length and frequency, to the point where executives spend an average of nearly 23 hours a week in meetings, up from less than ten hours in the 1960s.[99] Tony Prophet, the chief equality officer at Salesforce, thinks meetings offer a prime opportunity for change. Meetings are filled with 'thousands of moments' that reflect the culture of an organisation and the culture of more or less inclusion. Tony likes to ask people to think about the last meeting they were in. He asks us to reflect on some key questions.

- *Who spoke?*
- *Who took the majority of the airtime?*
- *Who was checking their messages when a certain person was talking and started paying attention when someone else was talking?*
- *Who threw an idea at the table that wasn't received as a great idea and ten minutes later, who else put the same idea on the table and all of a sudden, it's an incredible idea?*
- *Who interrupted?*
- *Who was interrupted?*
- *Who did you not hear from?*
- *Who got invited to the meeting?*
- *Who didn't get invited?*

In other words, we need to pay attention to how inclusive our meetings are and make changes where we see an opportunity for greater inclusion. Small and subtle shifts in how meetings are run can make an outsized difference to company culture.

"Meetings are filled with 'thousands of moments' that reflect the culture of an organisation and the culture of more or less inclusion."

If you want to improve how inclusive your meetings are, consider applying the principles below.

Better Listening: Most of us think faster than other people speak, creating the potential for significant mind wandering. To make matters worse, we are not as good at listening to some people versus other people. Being a better listener also tunes us in to whose voices are being discounted or muted.

Amplifying Other People: Although it is tempting to seek approval for our own ideas, it is much more powerful to recognise the good suggestions of other people. In meetings, explicitly look for and publicly note the contributions of others, especially those in the minority.

Speaking Order: One easy way to redesign meetings is to think about who is speaking when and in which order. Is it always the same person chairing team meetings? Who tends to speak first or the most in meetings? Consider rotating your meeting chair and who presents on certain topics and in what order.

Flexible input: Not everyone enjoys speaking in public as much as other people. Consider allowing for written input to meetings, as well as verbal. A good example comes from the software engineering company Ultranauts, who have 75 percent of employees on the autism spectrum. They record and transcribe all their meetings and allow employees to submit written input ahead of time.

Clarify Communication

Daily communication between colleagues is another area where inclusion can shine or be diminished. Social psychologist Justin Kruger and behavioural scientist Nick Epley have shown how most people overestimate the accuracy of their communication. In 2005, they ran a study where they had participants read a series of statements and they were told to communicate with a range of emotions, including: sarcasm; seriousness; anger; or sadness.[100] They did this either by email, as a voice recording, or face-to-face. They were asked how accurate they thought other people would be in decoding the tone of their statements. Overall, the communicators thought that other people would be pretty accurate in decoding their messages. The researchers showed these statements to other people and asked them to actually label the tone of the communication.

As you can see from the chart below, people overestimated their accuracy on every dimension. The worst discrepancy, however, was with email. Email carries no non-verbal information, tone of voice or other para-linguistic cues. But when people are writing their emails, they 'hear' them in the correct tone. You may not even know there is miscommunication. When it comes to important messages you draft, never simply read it to yourself in your head. Ask another person to read it out loud to you. Think about how it sounds and ask them what they think you mean. Remember to consider the emotional tone of your emails as much as the intellectual content.

EGOCENTRISM OVER EMAIL COMMUNICATION

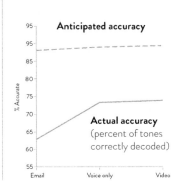

Source: Kruger, J., Epley, N., Parker, J., & Ng, Z. (2005). Egocentrism over e-mail: Can people communicate as well as they think? Journal of Personality and Social Psychology, 89, 925-936

Prioritise Mental Health

The COVID-19 pandemic has had a major effect on mental health and wellbeing globally. Many of us are facing new challenges that can be stressful, overwhelming and cause difficult emotions. Public health actions, such as social distancing can make us feel isolated and lonely, which have been shown to increase stress and anxiety. In the US, a large study from the JAMA Network found that there has been a three-fold increase in depression during the pandemic.[101] During 2020, suicide rates in Japan rose for the first time in 11 years, with the numbers showing women as being particularly vulnerable. In response, Japan has appointed a Minster of Loneliness with the goal of finding ways to reduce isolation as the world continues to grapple with the fallout of the pandemic. Businesses need to be as aware as governments of the mental health impacts on their employees.

It is not only mass global events that can trigger mental health issues. Researchers from Harvard and Stanford analysed decades of survey data and found that stressful jobs contribute to lower one's life expectancy.[102] It has also been found in a recently published study in the Journal of Racial and Ethnic Health Disparities that White men are more likely to face depression associated with stressful life events than Black men or women of any race.[103] The reason suggested in the research is that they have dealt with fewer stressful events in their life and therefore, lack the coping mechanisms and support systems that develop when overcoming hardship. The combination of a stressful work environment combined with mass global trauma is a toxic mix for a generation of professionals who will require careful navigation from business leaders.

Build Resilience

The good news is that there are reliable ways to build greater resilience in the workplace. Social support and reflective or spiritual practice are proven and effective coping mechanisms for dealing with stress.[104] The daily practice of being grateful has been found to ease depression, manage appetite, and enhance sleep.[105] One practical step could be to introduce a gratitude exercise for a specific day of the week, where team members share positive events that have happened, or mention individuals who they are grateful for. Some firms have created a shared record where team members note one thing for which they are grateful every day. Challenge your team to do it for three weeks straight. At the end of the three weeks, have your team reflect on their mood and productivity. Building in wellbeing practices to your work routine, such as a weekly time of reflection, opportunities for celebration and regular social support is wise business planning. It also allows the space for individuals to develop their inner lives, in the midst of busy and at times, stressful outer lives. Creating this space and time for inner work, contributes to a more inclusive working environment.

"Allow the space for individuals to develop their inner lives, in the midst of busy and at times, stressful outer lives."

More Movement

Wellbeing at work is about taking care of the whole person, the mind and the body. According to the University of Cambridge, being sedentary is as dangerous as being obese.[106] In a recent study, the school found that a lack of exercise accounts for twice as many deaths as obesity among European males. Another study published in the Annals of Internal Medicine found that the harmful effects of prolonged sedentary lifestyles persist, even with periods of intermittent exercise. One way to help your team get on their feet more is by offering standing desks. This is especially important when people are working from home and may be stuck at the kitchen table, rather than a well-designed office desk and chair. Another effective technique is moving meetings off cognitively draining video conferencing to 'walk and talk' meetings. Bringing movement to work has been shown to have several beneficial consequences. Not only are we improving our physical health, Stanford researchers found that our brains are 81 percent more creative when walking as opposed to sitting.[107]

Formalise Mentoring

Mentoring programs are one of the most effective ways to increase diversity and inclusion at work. Harvard Professors Dobbin and

Kalev looked at more than 800 companies to see how different diversity programs affected the proportions of ethnic minorities and women in management.[108] The results were impressive. Mentoring programs make companies' managerial levels significantly more diverse. On average, they boost the representation of Black, Hispanic and Asian women, and Hispanic and Asian men, by nine to 24 percent.

While White men tend to find mentors on their own, women and minorities more often need help from formal programs. One reason, as Georgetown's business school dean David Thomas discovered in his research on mentoring, is that White male executives don't feel comfortable reaching out informally to young women and minority men. Yet they are eager to mentor assigned mentees, and women and minorities are often the first to sign up for mentors. In 2020, Equality Group research found that more than half (55 per cent) of UK professionals did not know how to successfully build personal and professional relationships that would help progress them in their careers.[109] In addition, 30 percent of younger professionals, aged 18-24, compared to only 15 percent of older professionals felt that personal and professional relationships were more helpful in securing their first job than their academic achievements. Despite the well-documented benefits of mentoring on diversity, only ten percent of the 800 companies analysed by Dobbin and Kalev had formal programs. This represents a significant opportunity for more structured mentoring programs at work to help close the diversity gap.

To achieve even greater impact, it is worth considering a reverse mentoring programme. Turning the traditional mentoring model on its head, experienced colleagues are mentored by a younger or minority group colleague. The global consultancy EY has used reverse mentoring to tackle the problem of "out-of touch male executives", helping to create a cultural shift in how the company operates.[110] Reverse mentoring schemes which pair young women or ethnic minorities with senior male executives have been recognised as being instrumental in changing company-wide attitudes to recruitment and flexible working. Many other firms have introduced this concept with excellent outcomes including Microsoft, Linklaters and General Electric.

MENTORING
EXERCISE

Maya Angelou and Oprah Winfrey attend Surprise Oprah!
A Farewell Spectacular at the United Centre on May 17, 2011
in Chicago, Illinois. Oprah has expressed the power of mentorship
in her own words: "I've been blessed to have Maya Angelou as my
mentor, mother, sister and friend since my early 20s.
She was there for me always, guiding me through some of
the most important years of my life."

REFLECT

Who has been a mentor to you in your education, career
or life more broadly?

How has their advice shaped you or a certain chapter in your life?

Which of their words or actions meant the most to you?

What qualities made them such an important influence on you?

ACT

Take a moment of gratitude for your mentor(s) and consider sending
them a message of thanks today.

If you have never had a mentor, consider who has supported you in your
life. Although they may not have formally been called a mentor, there
are often people who have been positive influences on us and offered
the right words of encouragement or advice at a critical time. Consider
sending them a note of thanks today.

Have you ever mentored someone? Who could you mentor this year? If
your company doesn't offer this as part of a formal program, could you
help to start one?

A FINAL MESSAGE
FOR YOUR JOURNEY

The message that I want to leave with you for your journey ahead is inspired by the civil rights campaigner Martin Luther King Jr.:

"The arc of the moral universe is long, but it bends toward justice."

The diversity, equity and inclusion journey is a long one. It takes collaboration, creativity and empathy. There are many rewards along the way, but there are also stumbling blocks and setbacks. Keeping in mind the long term vision for justice and equality is essential.

In an age where technological advancements often appear to be outstripping all other forms of evolution, our growing awareness and collective consciousness is also rapidly emerging. Many people are becoming more aware of one another and of our environment. Developing our creativity and bravery at work is an essential part of this evolution.

When we talk about social sustainability in business, we are talking about work that supports, develops, rewards and nurtures people more fully. We are also talking about business that effectively combines the priorities of profit with those of purpose. When we harness greater levels of human talent and potential at work, there are outsized business benefits. With more inclusive innovations from diverse teams like those at J&J, and from inclusive leaders, like Satya Nadella, we create a win-win world.

On your journey, keep in mind this vision. A vision of our fullest human potential and collective development. A vision for work that is meaningful, purposeful and connected irrespective of gender, race, creed or ability.

CONTACT
THE AUTHOR

Website
www.hephzipemberton.com
www.equality.group

LinkedIn
https://www.linkedin.com/in/hephzi-pemberton/
https://www.linkedin.com/company/equalitygroupglobal

Twitter
https://twitter.com/hephzipemberton
https://twitter.com/equalitygroupgl

Instagram
https://www.instagram.com/hephzipemberton/
https://www.instagram.com/equalitygroupglobal/

Facebook
https://www.facebook.com/hephzi.pemberton
https://www.facebook.com/equalitygroupglobal

CHAPTER QUOTATION AND IMAGE REFERENCES

Chapter 1
Great Thunberg: born 2003, Swedish environmental activist
Photo credit: Daniele COSSU / Shutterstock

Chapter 2
Dr Christiana Ayoka Mary Thorpe: Sierra Leonean social activist and educationalist
Photo credit: Glasshouse Images 1967 / Shutterstock

Chapter 3
Barack Obama: former American president
Photo credit: K2 images / Shutterstock

Chapter 4
Peter Drucker: leadership and management expert
Photo credit: Everett Collection / Shutterstock

Chapter 5
Dolly Chugh: associate professor, New York University, Stern School of Business
Photo credit: VINCENT LAFORET/AFP via Getty Images

Chapter 6
Verna Myers: Vice President, Inclusion Strategy, Netflix
Photo credit: rightclickstudios / Shutterstock

Chapter 7
Teresa Amabile: research professor, Harvard University
Photo credit: FG/Bauer-Griffin/Getty Images

Chapter 8

Kathrine Switzer: American marathon runner, author and television commentator
Photo credit: Leon Neal/Getty Images

Chapter 9

Thomas a Kempis: 1380-1471, German-Dutch canon, of the late Medieval period and the author of The Imitation of Christ, one of the most popular and best-known Christian devotional books.
Photo credit: David Walter Banks/For The Washington Post via Getty Images

Chapter 10

Maya Angelou: 1951 – 2014, American poet, memoirist and civil rights activist. She published seven autobiographies, three books of essays, several books of poetry and is credited with a list of plays, movies, and television shows spanning more than 50 years.
Photo credit: Daniel Boczarski/Getty Images

REFERENCES
AND RESEARCH

The latest research about inclusion, diversity and equity from a range of academic institutions and business organisations, up to and including Q1 2021 has been included.

The majority of studies about diversity topics centre around the visible diversity characteristics of gender and race. Wherever possible, the author has tried to cite research about broader diversity demographic characteristics. However, there is a distinct shortage of robust research around disability, social mobility, sexuality and neurodiversity. There is also an outsized focus on the US and Europe in the current literature, which does not reflect the full global picture of the topic.

The author hopes is that during the coming years, there will be an increased body of research which will provide relevant updates to the chapters in this book and broaden the focus of the discussion further.

List of research cited
1. Equality Group, 2021.
2. Diversity Wins, McKinsey, 2020.
3. Diverse Leadership Teams Boost Innovation, BCG, 2018.
4. Nigel Morris, Harriet Harman: *If only it had been Lehman Sisters,* Independent.
5. Matthew Syed, Rebel Ideas: *The Power of Diverse Thinking,* (John Murray, 10 Sept 2019).
6. Gallup, Workplace Insight, 2017
7. Supriya Garikipati and Uma Kambhampati, *Leading the Fight Against the Pandemic: Does Gender 'Really' Matter?* (June 3, 2020), available at SSRN.
8. Equality Group, *#MeToo & #MenToo: Narrowing the gender gap,* March 2019.

9. Dolly Chugh, *The Person You Mean to Be: How Good People Fight Bias* (2019).

10. Khalil Smith, *Designing Leadership Models That Actually Work With Andrea Derler And Kamila Sip: The NLI Interview,* Forbes (April 2020).

11. Newsroom, Satya Nadella: *When empathy is good for business,* Morning Future, June 2018.

12. Julie Sweet and Ellyn Shook, *Getting To Equal 2020,* Accenture Report.

13. Higgins, E. T., *Promotion and prevention: Regulatory focus as a motivational principle in M. P. Zanna (Ed.)., Advances in experimental Social Psychology* Vol. 30 (1998) pp. 1-46.

14. Ronald S. Friedman and J. Forster, *The Effects of Promotion and Prevention Cues on Creativity,* Journal of Personality and Social Psychology Vol. 81, No. 6, pp. 1001-1013 Keller, J. et al. *Prevention-focused self-regulation and aggressiveness* ☆. Journal of Research in Personality 42 (2008): 800-820.; Trawalter, S., & Richeson, J. A. (2006) *Regulatory focus and executive function after interracial interactions.* Journal of Experimental Social Psychology, Vol. 42, No.3, pp. 406–412. https://doi.org/10.1016/j.jesp.2005.05.008

15. Butz, D. A., & Plant, E. A. (2009). *Prejudice control and interracial relations: The role of motivation to respond without prejudice.* Journal of Personality, 77(5), 1311–1341. https://doi.org/10.1111/j.1467-6494.2009.00583.x; Keon West and Katy Greenland, *Beware of "reducing prejudice": imagined contact may backfire if applied with a prevention focus,* Journal of Applied Social Psychology (2016) Vol. 46, No. 2, pp. 583-592

16. Bem, S. L., & Bem, D. J, *Does sex-biased job advertising "aid and abet" sex discrimination?* Journal of Applied Social Psychology, (1973) Vol. 3, No. 1, 6–18 https://doi.org/10.1111/j.1559-1816.1973.tb01290.x; Gastil, J, *Generic pronouns and sexist language: The oxymoronic character of masculine generics.* Sex Roles: A Journal of Research, (1990) Vol. 23, No. 11-12, pp. 629–643. https://doi.org/10.1007/BF00289252; Stout, J. G., & Dasgupta, N., *When he doesn't mean you: Gender-exclusive language as ostracism.* Personality and Social Psychology Bulletin, (2011) vol. 37, no. 6, pp. 757–769 https://doi.org/10.1177/0146167211406434.

17. Alison J. Patev et al., *College Students' Perceptions of Gender-Inclusive Language Use Predict Attitudes Toward Transgender and Gender Nonconforming Individuals,* Journal of Language and Social Psychology, (2018), vol. 38, no. 3 pp. 329-352.

18. Sczesny, S., Formanowicz, M., & Moser, F., *Can gender-fair language reduce gender stereotyping and discrimination?,* Frontiers in Psychology, (2016) Vol. 7, Article 25. https://doi.org/10.3389/fpsyg.2016.00025

19. Cisgender (sometimes cissexual, often abbreviated to simply cis) is a term for people whose gender identity matches their sex assigned at birth. For example, someone who identifies as a woman and was assigned female at birth is a cisgender woman. The term cisgender is the opposite of the word transgender.

20. Lift Every Voice: *The Biden Plan for Black America, 2020.* https://joebiden.com/blackamerica/

21. Equality Group, *BAME Boss: Ethnic Minority Aspirations of Being on the Board,* January 2019 Report.

22. Mendoza-Denton, R., Shaw-Taylor, L., Chen, S., & Chang, E., *Ironic effects of explicit gender prejudice on women's test performance.* Journal of Experimental Social Psychology, (2009) Vol. 45, No. 1, pp. 275–278. https://doi.org/10.1016/j.jesp.2008.08.017

23. Offermann, L. R., Basford, T. E., Graebner, R., Jaffer, S., De Graaf, S. B., & Kaminsky, S. E. (2014). *See no evil: Color blindness and perceptions of subtle racial discrimination in the workplace.* Cultural Diversity and Ethnic Minority Psychology, Vol. 20, No. 4, pp. 499–507. https://doi.org/10.1037/a0037237

24. Brene Brown, *Daring Greatly* (2015). https://www.waterstones.com/book/daring-greatly/brene-brown/9780241257401

25. Problems of Monetary Management: the U.K. experience, Charles Goodhart, 1975

26. "Improving Ratings". Marilyn Strathern 1997

27. Karen Brown, *To Retain Employees, Focus on Inclusion - Not Just Diversity,* Harvard Business Review (2018)

28. Stonewall, *LGBT in Britain,* Work Report (2018).

29. Equality Group, *Authenticity at Work: the importance of being yourself at work,* June 2019 Report.

30. Equality Group, *LGBTQ+ Lens Investing for the 2020s.* (2021). https://www.equality.group/lgbt-a-new-frontier-report

31. Ibid.

32. Katrin Auspurg et al., *Why Should Women Get Less? Evidence on the Gender Pay Gap from Multifactorial Survey Experiments,* American Sociological Review (2017) Vol. 82; Milkman, Katherine L et al. *What happens before? A field experiment exploring how pay and representation differentially shape bias on the pathway into organisations.* The Journal of applied psychology vol. 100,6 (2015): 1678-712; Bruckmüller, S., Ryan, M. K., Rink, F., & Haslam, S. A. (2014). *Beyond the glass ceiling: The glass cliff and its lessons for organisational policy.* Social Issues and Policy Review, 8(1), 202–232 https://doi.org/10.1111/sipr.12006; Ryan, Allison & Patrick, Helen & Shim, Sungok. (2005). *Differential Profiles of Students Identified by Their Teacher as Having Avoidant, Appropriate, or Dependent Help-Seeking Tendencies in the Classroom.* Journal of Educational Psychology. 97. 275-285. 10.1037/0022-0663.97.2.275.

33. Anthony F. Heath, Valentina Di Stasio, *Racial Discrimination in Britain, 1969-2017: a meta-analysis of field experiments on racial discrimination in the British labour market,* The British Journal of Sociology (2019), Vol. 70, No. 5, pp. 1774-1798.

34. Equality Group, Micropositives: *The little things that do a lot* (2020).

35. For an example inclusion and diversity commitment text outline refer to: https://www.equality.group/our-values

36. Iris Bohnet, *What Works: Gender Equality by Design* (2018).

37. Ibid.

38. Brandon Oto, *When thinking is hard: managing decision fatigue,* PubMed (2012).

39. Edmondson, Amy & Lei, Zhike. (2014). *Psychological Safety: The History, Renaissance, and Future of an Interpersonal Construct.* Annual Review of Organisational Psychology and Organisational Behavior. 1. 23-43. 10.1146/annurev-orgpsych-031413-091305.

40. PWC, *Are you missing millions,* (2019).

41. Equileap, *Gender Equality Global Report & Ranking,* (2019).

42. Mckinsey, *Focusing on what works for diversity in the workplace,* (2017).

43. Facebook, https://managingbias.fb.com/

44. Noon, *Pointless Diversity Training* (2017); Pearson, Dovidio, & Gaertner, *The nature of contemporary prejudice* (2009).

45. Becker & Wright, *Yet another dark side of chivalry* (2011).

46. Bezrukova et al., *A Meta-Analytical Integration of Over 40 Years of Research on Diversity Training Evaluation* (2016).

47. Atewologun, Cornish, & Tresh, *'Unconscious bias training'* (2018).

48. Dobbin & Kalev, (2016) ; Dobbin, Kalev & Kelly (2007); Kalev, Dobbin, Kelly 2006 ; Noon, 2018; West & Eaton (2019)

49. Bezrukova et al., *A Meta-Analytical Integration of Over 40 Years of Research on Diversity Training Evaluation* (2016).

50. Trust for London, https://www.trustforlondon.org.uk/ publications/annualreview2019/

51. Freya Williams, *Green Giants: How Smart Companies Turn Sustainability Into Billion-Dollar Businesses,* (2018).

52. Dolly Chugh, *The Person You Mean To Be,* (2019).

53. Robert B.Cialdini, Carl A.Kallgren, Raymond R.Reno, *A Focus Theory of Normative Conduct,* (1991).

54. Edward H. Chang, Katherine L. Milkman, *Dolly Chugh and Modupe Akinola, Diversity Thresholds,* (2019).

55. JP Morgan, *Workforce Composition Disclosure,* 2020

56. Priyanka Dwivedi, Aparna Joshi and Vilmos F. Misangyi, *Gender-Inclusive Gatekeeping,* (2018).

57. For the purpose of this chapter I refer to "I&D taskforce" although companies have different names for the same group. Ultimately, the function is more important than the name.

58. Dobbin and Kalev, *Why Diversity Programs Fail,* (2016).

59. Gallup *Workplace Study,* 2020

60. Equality Group, *Authenticity at Work,* (2019).

61. Glassdoor, *Diversity & Inclusion study* (2019).

62. Deloitte, *The Reality Gap,* (2017).

63. Teresa Amabile, *The Progress Principle,* (2014).

64. Kapor Center, *The 2017 Tech Leavers Study,* (2017).

65. Equality Group, *BAME Boss*, (2019).

66. Laura Wronski, CNBC|SurveyMonkey poll: International Women's Day (2020).

67. Sheryl Sandberg, *Lean in: Women, Work, and the Will to Lead*, 2013

68. Emilio J. Castilla, *Accounting for the Gap*, 2015

69. Janice Madden, *Performance-Support Bias and the Gender Pay Gap among Stockbrokers*, Gender & Society (2012), Vol. 26, No. 3, pp. 488-518.

70. Melissa Phillippi, *Overcoming Challenges of the Idiosyncratic Rater Effect* (2019).

71. Scullen, S. E., Mount, M. K., & Goff, M. (2000). *Understanding the latent structure of job performance ratings.* Journal of Applied Psychology, 85(6), 956–970. https://doi.org/10.1037/0021-9010.85.6.956

72. Bakker, A. B., Demerouti, E., & Euwema, M. C. (2005). *Job Resources Buffer the Impact of Job Demands on Burnout.* Journal of Occupational Health Psychology, 10(2), 170–180. https://doi.org/10.1037/1076-8998.10.2.170

73. Aleksandra Luksyte and Derek Avery, *Exploring burnout and work-family facilitation as factors influencing why and when relational demography diminishes employee citizenship,* Journal of Occupational and Organisational Psychology (2014), Vol. 88, No. 4.

74. Linda Babcock, Maria P. Recalde, Lisa Vesterlund, *Gender Differences in the Allocation of Low-Promotability Tasks: The Role of Backlash* (2017).; Babcock et al., Laurie Weingart, *Gender Differences in Accepting and Receiving Requests for Tasks with Low Promotability,* American Economic Review (2017), Vol. 107, No. 3.; Guarino, C. M., & Borden, V. M. H. (2017). *Faculty service loads and gender: Are women taking care of the academic family? Research in Higher Education* (2017) Vol. 58, No. 6, pp. 672–694.https://doi.org/10.1007/s11162-017-9454-2; Mitchell, Sara & Hesli, Vicki. (2013). *Women Don't Ask? Women Don't Say No? Bargaining and Service in the Political Science Profession.* PS: Political Science & Politics. Vol. 46, No.2. https://www.researchgate.net/publication/259431711_Women_Don%27t_Ask_Women_

Don%27t_Say_No_Bargaining_and_Service_in_the_
Political_Science_Profession

75. Miller, Candace & Roksa. Josipa, *Balancing Research and Service in Academia: Gender, Race, and Laboratory Tasks.* Gender & Society (2019). Vol. 34, No. 1.

76. Katie Juran, *Another step forward: Adobe pay and opportunity parity,* Adobe blog (2020).

77. Leaper, C., & Ayres, M. (2007). *A meta-analytic review of moderators of gender differences in adults' talkativeness, affiliative, and assertive speech.* Personality & Social Psychology Review, 11, 328-363.

78. Mehl, M. R., & Pennebaker, J. W. *The Sounds of Social Life* (2003).

79. Rob Kelly, *Ten Samples of an Effective EEO Statement* (2017).

80. Andreas Leibbrandt & John A. List, *Do EEO Statements Backfire,* (2018).

81. Matt Krentz, Justin Dean, Jennifer Garcia-Alonso, Miki Tsusaka, and Elliot Vaughn, *Fixing the Flawed Approach to Diversity,* BCG (2019).

82. For a clear and editable anti-discrimnation and anti-harassment policy template, please refer to this template on Workable, https://resources.workable.com/anti-discrimination-policy, which can be tailored to organisations of any size.

83. Jon Miller and Lucy Parker, *Open For Business: Strengthening the economic case* (2019).

84. OUTstanding research, (2019).

85. Caroline Vagneron, *Three ways to make LGBT-friendly policies work at work,* World Economic Forum (2017).

86. World Bank Group, Women, Business and the Law 2020.

87. EEOC, US, (2013).

88. HBR, *Diversity and Inclusion,* (2020).

89. Mercer Global Parental Leave Report: *Organisations Expand Policies to Accommodate Needs of Workforce* (2016). https://www.uk.mercer.com/newsroom/global-parental-leave-report-20160.html

90. Michelle Budig, *The fatherhood bonus and the motherhood penalty: Parenthood and the gender gap in pay,* Third Way (2014).

91. Pia S. Schober, *Parental Leave and Domestic Work of Mothers*

and Fathers: A Longitudinal Study of Two Reforms in West Germany, 2014.

92. Flouri, E., & Buchanan, A., *The role of father involvement in children's later mental health*. Journal of Adolescence (2003), Vol. 26, No. 1, 63–78.

93. EMW Law, 2020.

94. Twanley, Katherine & Pia, Schober. *Shared Parental Leave: Exploring Variations in Attitudes, Eligibility, Knowledge and Take-up Intentions of Expectant Mothers in London*. Journal of Social Policy, Vol. 48, No.2 (2019): pp. 387-407.

95. PwC *US Remote Work Survey*, January 2021.

96. Cristian L. Deszö, David Gaddis Ross, *Does female representation in top management improve firm performance? A panel data investigation*, Strategic Management Journal (2012), Vol. 33, No. 9, pp. 1072-1089.

97. Cloverpop, *Hacking Diversity with Inclusive Decision Making* (2018). https://www.cloverpop.com/hubfs/Whitepapers/Cloverpop_Hacking_Diversity_Inclusive_Decision_Making_White_Paper.pdf.

98. Katherine Phillips, Gregory B. Northcraft, and Margaret Neale, *Surface-Level Diversity and Decision-Making in Groups: When Does Deep-Level Similarity Help?* Group Processes and Intergroup Relations, SAGE Publications, 2006, Vol. 9 No. 4, pp.467-482. https://hal.archives-ouvertes.fr/hal-00571629/document

99. Rogelberg, Steven & Scott, Cliff & Kello, John. (2007). *The Science and Fiction of Meetings*. MIT Sloan Management Review. Vol. 48, No. 2.

100. Kruger, J., Epley, N., Parker, J., & Ng, Z.-W. (2005). *Egocentrism over e-mail: Can we communicate as well as we think?* Journal of Personality and Social Psychology, Vol. 89, No. 6, pp. 925–936. https://doi.org/10.1037/0022-3514.89.6.925.

101. Ettman CK, Abdalla SM, Cohen GH, Sampson L, Vivier PM, Galea S., *Prevalence of Depression Symptoms in US Adults Before and During the COVID-19 Pandemic*, JAMA Netw Open. 2020; Vol. 3 No. 9.

102. Joel Goh, Jeffrey Pfefer and Stefanos Zenits, *Exposure To*

Harmful Workplace Practices Could Account For Inequality In Life Spans Across Different Demographic Groups, Health Affairs (2015), Vol. 34, No. 10.

103. Assari, S., Lankarani, M.M., *Association Between Stressful Life Events and Depression; Intersection of Race and Gender.* J. Racial and Ethnic Health Disparities 3, pp. 349–356 (2016).

104. Ozbav et al., Social Support and Resilience to Stress, Psychiatry Vol. 4, No. 5 (2007), pp. 35-40. ; Kathleen Brewer-Smyth et al., *Could spirituality and religion promote stress resilience in survivors of childhood trauma?* Issues in mental health nursing vol. 35,4 (2014): pp. 251-6.

105. Dickens, L., & DeSteno, D. (2016). *The grateful are patient: Heightened daily gratitude is associated with attenuated temporal discounting. Emotion,* 16(4), 421–425. https://doi.org/10.1037/emo0000176

106. Ekelund U. Et al., *American Journal of Clinical Nutrition;* 14 Jan 2015.

107. Marily Oppezzo and Daniel L. Schwartz, *Give Your Ideas Some Legs: The Positive Effect of Walking on Creative Thinking,* Journal of Experimental Psychology: Learning, memory and Cognition, (2014), Vol. 40, No. 4, pp. 1142-1152.

108. Frank Dobbin and Alexandra Kalev, *Why Diversity Programs Fail,* Harvard Business Review (2016).

109. Equality Group, *Connections at Work* (2020).

110. Reverse Mentoring, ACE Network, (2018).

Printed in Great Britain
by Amazon